MARKED
FOR MISSION

Youth in Action

Morehouse Publishing
NEW YORK · HARRISBURG · DENVER

ISBN-13: 978-0-8192-2936-6

Unless otherwise noted, the Scripture quotations contained herein are from the New Revised Standard Version Bible, copyright © 1989 by the Division of Christian Education of the National Council of Churches of Christ in the U.S.A. Used by permission. All rights reserved.

Morehouse Publishing, 4785 Linglestown Road, Suite 101,
    Harrisburg, PA 17112
Morehouse Publishing, 19 East 34th Street, New York, NY 10016
Morehouse Publishing is an imprint of Church Publishing Incorporated.
www.churchpublishing.org

Cover design by Laurie Klein Westhafer
Typeset by Beth Oberhholtzer

Library of Congress Cataloging-in-Publication Data

A catalog record of this book is available from the Library of Congress

ISPB-13: 978-0-8192-2936-6 (pbk.)
ISPB-13: 978-0-8192-2937-3 (ebook)

Printed in the United States of America

In thanksgiving for the life and ministry of Deacon Terry Star, youth minister and church leader, Standing Rock Indian Reservation, North Dakota (1973–2014)

May the Holy Spirit guide and strengthen you,
that in this, and in all things, you may do God's will
in the service of the kingdom of Christ. Amen.

"A Prayer for the Commitment to Christian Service," BCP, p. 420

Contents

Foreword

God loves you, and so do I. That's what this powerful little book is meant to say and teach. The art and practice of Christian living is grounded in a deep understanding that each of us is valued beyond imagining and that we reflect that in the way we love others.

We tend to think of love as a feeling, particularly in Western cultures, because it's hard to talk about in rational or thinking terms. Yet love is far more about how we act, even as it is known in "sighs too deep for words."[1] The roots of Judaism, Christianity, and Islam lie in cultures that understood the heart to be the seat of decision-making. It is why we understand justice to be love "in public"—the way communities and nations ensure that people are treated fairly. We learn that we are loved through the actions of people around us, beginning with being fed and clothed and comforted as infants. Through stories we begin to hear about the loving actions of people who came before us or live far away. When Christians are baptized, they claim very particular stories about how the love of God is present in this world, and they—we—keep learning about the depth of that love throughout our lives. We live in hope that our very lives show evidence of the love we know, and we take the example of Jesus of Nazareth as our primary teacher. Baptism is an act that joins us to his body present throughout the ages, and commits us to live in the ways he did. We all learn to do that

---

1. Romans 8:26

more effectively in community—joining together with others who share those baptismal commitments to keep discovering Love in the world around us.

The story or image that is most central to the lives of Christians is about God's overarching intent for all of creation—that it be a community of love, that acts in love and becomes more like the God we call Love. That means justice in society, peace-making where there is strife, and living in ways that help to sustain the rest of creation. We call that God's mission, and it's quite clearly what Jesus understood his job to be. His first public act of ministry (the word means service) was to read a story about that vision in his hometown synagogue:

> "The Spirit of the Lord is upon me,
>> because he has anointed me
>>> to bring good news to the poor.
> He has sent me to proclaim release to
> the captives
>> and recovery of sight to the blind,
>>> to let the oppressed go free,
> to proclaim the year of the Lord's favor."

And he rolled up the scroll, gave it back to the attendant, and sat down. The eyes of all in the synagogue were fixed on him. Then he began to say to them, "Today this scripture has been fulfilled in your hearing."[2]

He was reading from one of the Hebrew prophets, Isaiah, and it is a vision of healing and restoration that is repeated over and over in the Bible. Christians understand that our task is also

---

2. Luke 4:18–19

to show the world that "this scripture is being fulfilled" today as we share in this mission of God's.

Our lives in the world are meant to be offered and spent as agents of transformation toward that vision. Working for that transformation is what it means to be a Christian leader, and you will find helpful frameworks here (the promises of the Baptismal Covenant and the Five Marks of Mission) for reflection and even evaluation of our part in God's mission, both as individuals and as communities. In all we are and all we do, we are meant to live as part of the body of Christ, bringing that vision of wholeness and restored creation into being. We are to live as co-creators with God.

In baptism, we promise to share in God's life, and you will find here some images that may evoke new understandings of what that can look like: companion, witness, pilgrim, servant, ambassador, host, even sacrament. There are others as well, and you are encouraged to find some that help your journey! As you consider what it looks like to live as a godly companion or witness or even as a sacrament, think of it in terms of sharing, in God's life and the life of the world around you. A companion is one who shares bread—Jesus called himself the bread of life— this is both physical bread and spiritual bread, the very stuff that sustains our bodies from day to day and our whole beings for greater life. A witness shares stories and news about love experienced, and in doing so, shares hope. A servant (or minister) shares life with another, and shares the loads and burdens of life as well as the joys. A sacrament is a sharing of the holy through the stuff of creation—in ways that honor the very nature of all that God has created. How will you become such a sharer and partaker of the life of God?

May you continue to become one who knows Love deep within, and who shares that Love in all parts of the life that has been given to you. May you know yourself well-loved and blessed, and be a blessing to the world.

Katharine Jefferts Schori
XXVI Presiding Bishop

Acknowledgments

With thanks to all those who contributed prayers and stories, especially . . .

The Episcopal Youth Event Mission Planning Team, 2014

The Diversity and Ethnic Ministries Team
of The Episcopal Church

The Formation and Congregational Development Team
of The Episcopal Church

Introduction

You are sealed by the Holy Spirit in Baptism and marked as Christ's own for ever. Amen.

Book of Common Prayer, p. 308

You are marked for mission. Yes, YOU, a beloved child of God, are called to engage God's mission in the world. God knows it, the Church knows it, and you need to know it. But how does a teenager or young adult discover and engage that mission?

The Episcopal Youth Event 2014 Mission Planning Team began digging in on that very question at their first meeting in the spring of 2013. Those fourteen teenagers from across the church, from Hawaii to Massachusetts, to the Dominican Republic, to Minnesota, started building faithful community through studying scripture, participating in worship, and practicing prayer. They worked with their adult mentors to learn about the Anglican Marks of Mission, to renew their baptismal promises, and to share stories of when they felt God's presence in their lives. They all agreed that learning about our place in God's mission is a never-ending reveal; that if we are faithful in watching for what the Holy Spirit is stirring amongst us, we will be continually invited and inspired to participate and may be transformed again and again and again.

We shared our favorite scripture passages and explained why each of those passages had personal impact for us. And it was through those stories of faith and sorrow and joy and wonder that we came to better understand one another and what God was calling us to do together. A faithful community in action was born again and we engaged the business of hosting a new community of faithful high schoolers in Philadelphia, Pennsylvania, in July of 2014. A theme was discerned: "Marked for Mission," and the invitation to the wider church began. Sharon Ely Pearson from Church Publishing Incorporated graciously agreed to help develop this resource that would be a compilation of scripture, story, teaching, and prayer. This small volume is the EYE Mission Planning Team's loving gift to you— the Church.

In the fall of 2013 we invited youth, young adults, and the adults in ministry with them, to share their experiences of acting on their baptismal promises, living the Marks of Mission, inviting others to join them in action, being inspired by others to engage, and being transformed as followers of Jesus. The stories and prayers gathered here are but whispers of the greater story. It is our hope and prayer that you will adapt and adopt the practice of scripture, prayer, action, and story to help evangelize those who are so thirsty for Good News.

The sections that follow are designed to equip you with spiritual language and practice when engaging the ordinary and the extraordinary. Just as Jesus used the power of parables to make his point, we invite you to seek the sacred in everyday circumstances and share your stories of Jesus being revealed to you.

As a mother of young sons and as a youth minister, I have been amazed time and time again at how the Holy Spirit has been at work in my life, often not revealed to me until I shared the story of the miracle I witnessed. I don't always recognize the Kingdom moment at the time, but telling the stories (like when my three-year-old described what heaven was like before being born) helped my audience and me recognize the sacrament of his revelation . . . *I believe in the seen and the unseen* (The Nicene Creed).

And when my six-year-old was giving away water and lemonade during the HIV/AIDS fundraising bicycle ride past our rural home, only to donate his hundreds of dollars in tips to the Minnesota HIV/AIDS Foundation, I was stunned with his sense of care for a much greater community . . . *when I was thirsty you gave me water to drink* (Matthew 25:35).

A phone call in the late evening from a depressed young adult confessing that his life was so hopeless that he was about to drive himself off of a mountain in Colorado caused transformation in both of us. He stopped to call me because he remembered me saying in youth group that, "Nothing can separate you from God's love, and you can call me anytime if you need to be reminded." He called, we talked, he drove down safely, and called a suicide prevention hotline to get local and immediate help . . . *nor anything else in all creation, will be able to separate us from the love of God in Christ Jesus our Lord* (Romans 8:39).

It is our hope that this book will serve as a tool for equipping youth and young adults in recognizing the sacred and grace-filled moments of their own human experience, and share their stories with all the generations. It is intended as a beginning of a deeper sharing in the hopes that we will all respond to God's mission in the world through faithful action. Please join us!

Faithfully,
Bronwyn Clark Skov
Youth Ministries Missioner
The Episcopal Church

THE BAPTISMAL COVENANT

*O God, you have created all things by the power
of your Word, and you renew the earth by your
Spirit: Give now the water of life to those who thirst
for you, that they may bring forth abundant fruit
in your glorious kingdom; through Jesus Christ our
Lord. Amen.*

Book of Common Prayer, p. 290

The Baptismal Covenant (English)

Celebrant Do you believe in God the Father?
People I believe in God, the Father almighty,
creator of heaven and earth.

Celebrant Do you believe in Jesus Christ, the Son of God?
People I believe in Jesus Christ, his only Son, our Lord.
He was conceived by the power of the Holy Spirit
and was born of the Virgin Mary
He suffered under Pontius Pilate,
was crucified, died, and was buried.
He descended to the dead.
On the third day he rose again.
He ascended into heaven,
and is seated at the right hand of the Father.
He will come again to judge the living and the dead.

Celebrant Do you believe in God the Holy Spirit?
People I believe in the Holy Spirit,
the holy catholic Church,
the communion of saints,
the forgiveness of sins,
the resurrection of the body,
and the life everlasting.

Celebrant	Will you continue in the apostles' teaching and fellowship, in the breaking of bread, and in the prayers?
People	I will, with God's help.
Celebrant	Will you persevere in resisting evil, and, whenever you fall into sin, repent and return to the Lord?
People	I will, with God's help.
Celebrant	Will you proclaim by word and example the Good News of God in Christ?
People	I will, with God's help.
Celebrant	Will you seek and serve Christ in all persons, loving your neighbor as yourself?
People	I will, with God's help.
Celebrant	Will you strive for justice and peace among all people and respect the dignity of every human being?
People	I will, with God's help.

From the Book of Common Prayer, pp. 304–305

Alliance baptismale (French)

Le célébrant Croyez-vous en Dieu, le Père?
Le peuple Je crois en Dieu, le Père tout-puissant,
  Créateur du ciel et de la terre.

Le célébrant Croyez-vous en Jésus Christ, le Fils de Dieu?
Le peuple Je crois en Jésus Christ, son Fils unique,
Notre Seigneur,
  qui a été conçu du Saint-Esprit,
  est né de la Vierge Marie,
  a souffert sous Ponce Pilate,
  a été crucifié, est mort
    et a été enseveli,
  est descend aux enfers,
  le troisième jour est ressuscité des morts,
  est monté aux cieux,
  est assis à la droite de Dieu
  le Père tout-puissant,
  d'où il viendra juger les vivants et les morts.

Le célébrant Croyez-vous en l'Esprit Saint?
Le peuple Je crois en l'Esprit Saint.
  à la Sainte Eglise catholique
  à la communion des saints,
  á la remission des péchés,
  à la vie éternelle.

Le célébrant	Serez-vous assidus à l'enseignements des apôtres, à la communion fraternell, à la fraction du pain et aux prières?
Le peuple	Oui, avec l'aide de Dieu.
Le célébrant	Persévérerez-vous dans votre résistance au mal et, si vous péchez, promettez-vous de vous repentir et de revenir au Seigneur?
Le peuple	Oui, avec l'aide de Dieu.
Le célébrant	Proclamerez-vous, tant par vos paroles que Par votre exemple, la Bonne Nouvelle de Dieu Manifestée en Jésus Christ?
Le peuple	Oui, avec l'aide de Dieu.
Le célébrant	Rechercherez-vous, pur le server, le Christ dans les personnes que vous rencontrerez, et aimerez-vous votre prochain comme vous-mêmes?
Le peuple	Oui, avec l'aide de Dieu.
Le célébrant	Etes-vous prêts à lutter pour la justice et la paix parmi tous les peuples et à respecter la dignité de chaque être humain?
Le peuple	Oui, avec l'aide de Dieu.

Kab Ke Cog Lus Ntxuav Plig (Hmong)

Leej Choj Koj puas ntsee txog Leej Txiv Tswv Ntuj?

Sawv daws Kuv ntseeg txog Tswv Ntuj, yog Leej Txiv tus muaj hwj chim loj tas nrho, yog tus tsim ntuj tsim teb.

Leej Choj Koj puas ntseeg txog Yes Xus, uas yog Tswv Ntuj Leej Tub?

Sawv daws Kuv ntseeg txog Yes Xus Pleev, yog Tswv Ntuj Leej Tub, yog peb tus Huab Tais. Leej Ntuj Plig Ntshiab ua kom nws xeeb los ua neeg, nws yug ntawm Leej Ntshiab Mab Liab los. Lub caij Pis Las Tos ua nom nws raug luag hima, tsim txom tuag thiab tau mus zwm av. Hnub peb nws sawv rov los. Nws tau nce mus saum ntuj, nws zaum ntawn Leej Txiv phab xis. Nws yuav rov los txiav txim rau cov neeg ciaj thiab neeg tuag.

Leej Choj Koj puas ntseeg txog Leej Ntuj Plig Ntshiab?

Sawv daws Kuv ntseeg txog Leej Ntuj Plig Ntshiab, lub koom txoos kas tos liv ntshiab, cov Leej Ntshiab, ntseeg txog kev daws txhaum, ntseeg txog lub cev yuav sawv rov los muaj txoj sia nyob mus li.

Leej Choj Koj puas zoo siab ua nws ib tug tub txib tshaj nws cov lo lus qhia, ntawn lub cim yug thiab kev thov ntuj?

Sawv daws Kuv zoo siab yuav ua, thov Tswv Ntuj pab.

Leej Choj	Koj puas tiv thaiv cov dab phem, thaum koj poob rau kev ua txhaum, lees txhaum thiab tig rov cuag Tswv Ntuj?
Sawv daws	Kuv yuav tiv thaiv, thov Tswv Ntuj pab.
Leej Choj	Koj puas kam tshaj Tswv Ntuj lo lus thiab nws tus cuj pwm zoo ntawm Leej Pleev Tswv Ntuj?
Sawv daws	Kuv kam tshaj, thov Tswv Ntuj pab.
Leej Choj	Koj puas nrhiav thiab pe hawm Leej Pleev hauv txhua tus tib neeg, nyiam cov nyob ze koj li koj nyiam koj?
Sawv daws	Kuv yuav nrhiav, thov Tswv Ntuj pab.
Leej Choj	Koj puas nrhiav kev ncaj ncees thiab sib haum xeeb rau txhua tus tib neeg, thiab hwm txhua tus tib neeg?
Sawv daws	Kuv nrhiav, thov Tswv Ntuj pab.

Pacto Bautismal (Spanish)

Celebrante	¿Crees en Dios Padre?
Pueblo	Creo en Dios Padre todopoderoso,
	creador del cielo y de la tierra.

Celebrante	¿Crees en Jesucristo, el Hijo de Dios?
Pueblo	Creo en Jesucristo, su único Hijo, nuestro Señor.
	Fue concebido por obra y gracia del
	Espíritu Santo
	Y nació de la Virgen María.
	Padeció bajo el poder de Poncio Pilato.
	Fue crucificado, muerto y sepultado.
	Descendió a los infiernos.
	Al tercer día resucitó de entre los muertos.
	Subió a los cielos,
	y está sentado a la diestra de Dios Padre.
	Desde allí ha de venir a juzgar a
	vivos y muertos.

Celebrante	¿Crees en Dios el Espíritu Santo?
Pueblo	Creo en el Espíritu Santo,
	la santa Iglesia católica,
	la comunión de los santos,
	el perdón de los pecados,
	la resurrección de los muertos,
	y la vida eterna.

Celebrante	¿Continuarás en la enseñanza y communion de los apóstoles, en la fracción del pan y en las oraciones?
Pueblo	Así lo hare, con el auxilio de Dios.
Celebrante	¿Perseverarás en resistir al mal, y cuando caigas en pecado, te arrepentirás y te volverás al Señor?
Pueblo	Así lo hare, con el auxilio de Dios.
Celebrante	¿Proclamarás por medio de la palabra y el ejemplo las Buenas Nuevas de Dios en Cristo?
Pueblo	Así lo hare, con el auxilio de Dios.
Celebrante	¿Buscarás y servirás a Cristo en todas las personas, amando a tu prójimo com a ti mismo?
Pueblo	Así lo hare, con el auxilio de Dios.
Celebrante	¿Lucharás por la justicia y la paz entre todos los pueblos, y respetarás la dignidad de todo ser humano?
Pueblo	Así lo hare, con el auxilio de Dios.

The Baptismal Covenant (Chinese)

聖洗禮誓約

主禮　你們是否相信上帝聖父？
會眾　**我信上帝，全能的聖父，是創造天地的主。**
主禮　你們是否相信上帝聖子耶穌基督？
會眾　**我信我主耶穌基督，是上帝的獨生子。**
　　　因聖靈的大能感孕，由童貞女馬利亞所生。
　　　他在本丟彼拉多手下受難，釘在十字架上，
　　　被害，埋葬。祂降在陰間，第三天祂復活，升天
　　　坐在聖父的右邊。祂必再臨，審判活人、死人。
主禮　你們是否相信上帝聖靈？
會眾　**我信聖靈，我信聖而公的教會，我信聖徒相通，**
　　　我信罪得赦免，我信身體復活，我信永生。
主禮　你們是否願意持守使徒的訓誨和團契生活，
　　　擘餅和禱告？
會眾　**我願意。求主幫助。**
主禮　你們是否願意堅決抵擋邪惡，若有過犯，願意悔改，
　　　歸回上帝？
會眾　**我願意。求主幫助。**
主禮　你們是否願意宣講上帝的道，
　　　以言行闡揚基督的福音？
會眾　**我願意。求主幫助。**
主禮　你們是否願意在眾人中尋求服事基度，
　　　並愛鄰如己？
會眾　**我願意。求主幫助。**
主禮　你們是否願意在人間力求正義與和平，
　　　並尊重每個人的尊嚴？
會眾　**我願意。求主幫助。**

I Will, With God's Help

Our Baptismal Covenant begins with an affirmation of our faith in the Trinity found in the Apostles' Creed. In response to the first three questions, as a community we acknowledge our belief in God as Creator, Jesus as Redeemer, and the Holy Spirit as the Sustainer. Together with the additional five questions, the Baptismal Covenant is primarily about God and the important relationship God establishes with us in baptism. It tells us who God is, and what God has done for us. It tells us that God loves us and calls us into relationship. God calls us to participate in God's self-giving love for the sake of the world. And to that we say, "I will, with God's help."

A covenant is a binding agreement that is freely entered into by two or more parties that may be individuals or groups of people. It is an important theme throughout Holy Scripture. God continually sought relationships with the people in the Old Testament: God's bow in the clouds was the sign of a covenant with Noah. God made a covenant with Abraham, in which God promised his descendants would be as numerous as the stars and they would have the Promised Land. God made a covenant with Moses that the people of Israel would be God's people, and God would be their God. This was to be lived out in terms of the Ten Commandments.

The new covenant is the new relationship with God given by Jesus to the apostles and through them to all who believe in Jesus (see the Book of Common Prayer, pp. 850–851). We live out our participation in the new covenant by sharing in the Holy Eucharist and in loving one another as Christ loved us (John 13:34–35).

The baptism of Jesus is one of the few incidents in his life that is mentioned in all four gospels (Matthew 3:13–17, Mark 1:9–11, Luke 3:21–22, and John 1:29–34). Baptism makes a person a member of Christ and a child of God. It is a radical sign of a new way of living one's life, a life that is sustained by the power of the Spirit that is Christ's.

Christian life begins with baptism, that ritual immersion in water "in the Name of the Father, and of the Son, and of the Holy Spirit." In the early church, to be baptized was to be "in Christ," to be members of His Body, the Church, and thus share a common way of life. Baptism was understood as a pledge, vow, covenant, or contract early in the history of the Christian Church. The very term sacrament meant an oath in Roman culture. When children of Christian parents were baptized, whether as part of the households mentioned in the New Testament or as children born into families that had been Christian for generations, the parents and baptismal sponsors made this pledge.

The Creeds were first developed as baptismal statements, and the Apostles' Creed serves as the chief individual profession of faith. As in the early days of the Church, today the baptismal candidate (or their sponsors) recites the Creed in response to three questions. A series of five questions have been added to the Creed to form the Baptismal Covenant in our Book of Common Prayer. These questions are about living as a Christian in daily life.

The first question quotes Acts 2:24, which describes the life of the early church and asks whether the candidate will also follow that pattern. The remaining questions move from the need for repentance to the need to proclaim the gospel, to serve others, and to work for justice, peace, and human dignity.

We share this new covenant with each other in Christ's name by living as Christ lived, with the help of the Holy Spirit. The Christian life is not an individual matter, a "me and God" relationship, but a membership in a body and a life of witness and service. It calls on us to act out our faith in specific ways. It is valuable to be reminded of that whenever there is a baptism, which is why the whole community shares in the renewal of our Baptismal Covenant as part of the baptismal liturgy.

In Action

Will you continue in the apostles' teaching and fellowship, in the breaking of bread, and in the prayers?

In the midst of my many childhood memories of church, there's one experience in particular that helped me to claim for myself the promises made for me in my Baptismal Covenant. The date was November 16, 2007, and I was in the backseat of my Rite 13 teacher's car, heading to the Barbara C. Harris Camp and Conference Center (BHC) for the Diocese of Massachusetts' annual Middle School Retreat. I was thirteen, in the seventh grade, and I never ever imagined that I would be writing this all down someday.

My seventh-grade self was very different from the person I am now. My main priority was to do well in school and make everyone around me happy, and to me that meant always doing everything exactly right. I was really shy, and spent most of my time doing homework, trying to blend in with everyone else, and worrying about what other people were thinking about me. So as you can imagine, I didn't have much confidence in myself at all—in fact, I was still trying to figure out who "myself" really was. And the same was true about my faith. Even though I had grown up going to church and Sunday school every week with my family, I had reached the point where I was trying to figure out my beliefs for myself, and decide what I thought about this whole religion thing.

Essentially, my goal was just to make it through middle school and try to be invisible for as much of it as I could.

I ended up going to that first retreat on a whim—my friend and I had promised each other that "I'll go if you go," and eventually we both signed up. And so we piled into the car on a Friday afternoon and drove two hours through the snow, up to a little camp in the New Hampshire woods that we had never been to before and didn't know anything about. I entered that retreat with pretty low expectations for the weekend: we would have fun, talk about God, and maybe meet a few people from other parishes.

As it turns out, I was completely unprepared for the effect that that retreat would have on me. I remember vividly every detail of the weekend—the names of the people in my small group, the table we sat at in the dining hall, even where I stood during worship. Because at that retreat, in my small group or at meals or during worship, I couldn't be invisible. The people I had met there wouldn't let me, because they cared about who I was and what I had to say. I had never experienced anything like that before; where everyone around me was not only the same age I was, but also of the same faith background. I had never worshipped with dance moves and a projection screen instead of a hymnal and organ. And I'd definitely never felt so close to God before.

So when Sunday afternoon rolled around and it was time for us to go back home, I didn't want to leave. I had just discovered this incredible community and a whole new side of myself, and I was afraid that all of it would disappear once I was back at school, as if the weekend had never happened, and I would go back to being my shy, normal self.

But that's not what happened. I never lost that feeling I had at the retreat. I went home having learned a lot about myself and about my faith. But more importantly, I found myself acting and thinking differently, even at school. It didn't really matter so much anymore what everyone else thought of me, because I knew that God would be with me no matter what. I started speaking up for myself more, because my small group had shown me that my voice was valuable. And I stopped trying to be somebody else when I finally realized that God had made me and loved me for who I was. I wasn't invisible anymore, and to my surprise, I loved it.

So the next summer, even though I had never even considered leaving home before, I decided to go to a week of camp at BCH. Since then I've been doing my best to listen to where God is calling me next, whether it be to do mission work in El Salvador, become a camp counselor, or share my faith journey with others.

If you had told me on November 16, 2007, that I would come to think of the upcoming weekend as one of the most formative experiences of my life, I would have called you crazy. If you had told me that during high school I would be on my parish's vestry or go to General Convention as a member of the Official Youth Presence, I would have just laughed at you. And if you had told me that I would someday willingly talk to a bunch of people about my faith, I probably would have questioned your sanity. Back then I didn't think I could be all of that, but I realize now that that person was there all along.

I would say that going to that retreat changed me, but it didn't—it just showed me that in order to proclaim the Good News of the Kingdom, I had to first be confident in using my own voice.

Sarah Neumann, Church of Our Redeemer, Lexington, Massachusetts

Will you persevere in resisting evil, and, whenever you fall into sin, repent and return to the Lord?

I am able to proudly respond with, "I will, with God's help." As a human being, I am bound to make mistakes and fall short of expectations on nearly a daily basis. God knows this, which is why He allows us to repent and forgives our sins. If He didn't, He would be awfully lonely up in heaven. Asking a teenager, or anyone for that matter, to resist all evil and temptations is asking a lot. God puts an enormous amount of faith in us, but He knows that we will occasionally fall short. The amazing part is that God will forgive us for anything; all we have to do is ask!

One of the problems I tend to have with this is using it as a safety net. It is too easy to think, "I know this is wrong, but I'm going to do it anyway and ask for forgiveness later since God forgives everything." If you know in the moment that what you are doing is going to call for an apology, then it is time to stop and rethink the situation. It is important to live in a way that would make God proud. Everyone falls down, and I am truly thankful for an amazing God who is always there to pick me back up again.

Madeline Carroll, All Saints Episcopal Cathedral, Wauwatosa, Wisconsin

There was a time in my life where I became egotistical because I was known as "the girl who participates in every event at church." I enveloped myself so much in the acknowledgments I received that I forgot the main purpose of my participation—to serve God. I changed for the better after suffering a bad experience, and now I work for two purposes: Serve God. Help others.

Tonie Renaud, Church of the Resurrection, Miami, Florida

The men in my family have always been the unlucky ones. It's a simple issue of math. We are outnumbered. And for me, the fact that all of my siblings are significantly older than I am has not helped. Add to this that my three sisters are the mature and disciplined ones in my family. Whenever I got into trouble, my mom would scold me, but it was my sisters who determined and dealt out punishment.

I don't imagine I ever really hated my sisters, but there were times when I said those words, "I hate you!" with passion and with tears of sadness and tears of anger rolling down my cheeks. But I was kid. I got hurt, and it hurt for a second or a minute or a day, and then I moved on.

In our spiritual journeys, God constantly allows us to see things in a new light, in a light of truth. And as I have continued to move on, I have seen more and more of the whole picture of my childhood. I have had the revelation that all that time that I spent judging my siblings for punishing me, I never really owned up to the fact that I had been in the wrong, and they had the right and loving desire to correct me.

But I also saw that just as I was judging my siblings, so too were they judging me. My siblings were disappointed in where they thought I was going to end up in my life. I struggled with this notion for a long while, but then things changed at some point. My siblings began responding differently to my life choices. They were so impressed with the man I was becoming and how I had matured. The praise came more frequently, as if every day I was learning how to be, and actually was becoming, a better person.

Frankly, this suspension of judgment and the removal of this stumbling block led me to new places I never thought I would or could reach. Currently, I am spending time in Maryland through the Episcopal Service Corps.

As a part of SMY work, I serve as the youth minister at an Episcopal church. And when I look around at all my young brothers and sisters in God, I find that I am reminded of my own childhood. I have to try very hard at times not to pass judgment on some of their actions and reactions. I pray they are not passing too much judgment on me. But I mostly pray that I have not been and that I will never be the same stumbling block in their lives that people, including myself, have been in my life.

For if I want them to learn anything, it is this: That the God of love is our only judge, and that as human beings we exist not to pass judgment and thereby increase human suffering. Never are we to be stumbling blocks, but we live today and until the end of our days so that we might be the ones who help others to remove these blocks to a life of faith, a life fully lived with God and in Christ.

Patrick Christopher Kangrga, Timonium, Maryland

Will you proclaim by word and example the Good News of God in Christ?

After I graduated college I was a bit lost in the world. I went to work at a local shop and went to church on Sunday, but there was something missing in my life. My bishop recommended that I look into a year of service to help with my discernment process. So I applied to the Episcopal Service Corps in Baltimore, Maryland.

For eleven months of my life I am able to live out the baptismal promises for what feels like all day, every day. I am living in an intentional Christian community, leading a life of prayer and reflection, as well as working towards social justice through my internship. Working with the youth ministries office, as well as the diocese, allows me to discover how I best proclaim the word. Not every moment has been smooth sailing, but I have felt God in my life more as each day passes.

Kate Riley, Emmanuel Episcopal Church, Cumberland, Maryland

When I look at the Baptismal Covenant, this question seems to be the most overlooked, in my opinion. In fact, I think it makes people more nervous than the other promises, even the ones that hold the baptized to high expectation, such as, "Will you strive for justice and peace among all people, and respect the dignity of every human being?" That seems like a challenge. Ironically, the most challenging and daunting promise is one of the simplest—go tell everyone about these great things God is doing in our lives! But that's the challenge. One must identify God's good work in their life.

I believe leadership is recognizing the skills you have, recognizing the skills needed in a situation, and if they match, step up and lead. This baptismal promise is directed to all of us, but in the 21st century, that kind of leadership is what we need with that promise. Those who have recognized God's deeds are called to tell people about them, and that is what I try to do.

In my own personal life, there have been many negative experiences, but later are seen as positive. Some have criticized me for my ministries in my parish because of my age, but later, these critics and I have become close, and I have developed spiritually more than I ever have. I have experienced the resurrection of Jesus, the good things coming from the bad things, and I tell people about it in the best way I know how as a high school student: in my youth group, on my blog, on my social media accounts, and many more ways! That's what that baptismal promise is about: stepping up, and preaching the good news once you have experienced it!

Thomas Alexander, St. Margaret's Episcopal Church,
Little Rock, Arkansas

Will you seek and serve Christ in all persons, loving your neighbor as yourself?

I live out this promise as best as I can in college. People come with baggage, and their struggles are completely valid, despite how trivial they may seem to others. By listening, and caring for everyone, I try and support others through the thick and thin. I have made some great friends this way, and I know I have done the right thing. I am living in the example of Christ by being compassionate to all people and caring for them as He does for us.

Ben Cowgill, St. Timothy's, Winston-Salem, North Carolina

I will.

Well . . . I will try. Sometimes, you know, it's actually quite difficult to find the divine in the kid who sits next to me in class popping gum incessantly throughout the entire lecture. The reality of the world, of human interaction, is that I do not like every person I meet. I do not immediately connect with every peer. I do not see Christ in all people right away, the second we meet, every time. Sometimes, I don't even remember to seek Christ in myself. But I know He is there, calling out to me, to you, waiting patiently for us to open our eyes just a bit wider and greet him like the old friend that he most certainly is. The thing is, before I can even begin to seek and serve Christ in every person that I meet, I have to make sure that I am seeking and serving the divine that lives within me. And that's hard, in the face of peer pressure and social expectations and my own self-criticism. It is a struggle we all face, and so I think the way I understand that baptismal promise is this: that in those moments when your eyes are just not quite open enough to see God in yourself or in the world around you, I will call out to you your own Godliness, because in doing so I will be reminded of my own, and then we can serve Christ together, in love and with grace.

So this is for me. For my sisters and my parents and all my family, blood and chosen. For my best friend. For the kid popping his gum next to me in lecture. For every person who's ever forgotten their own preciousness in the sight of God, or who sometimes thinks they are not worthy of God. I have something I want you to hear.

You are loved.

Let me repeat that. You are loved.

And you are perfect. Yes, you, who don't even completely know yourself and who sometimes feels like a total mess on stressed out Tuesday nights and who has a tiny inner voice wishing to be something other than you are. You're perfect. Christ lives within you. You are a chosen member of creation, designed by the gentle and meticulous hand of God for His own purposes in the world. You are made of stars, of hope and joy and the grace of the divine. Do not deny yourself the honor of meeting who you are meant to be, who you truly are in your heart of hearts. You are not bad, or wrong, or made incorrectly. You are perfect, just as you are: a marvelous piece of creation with whom God is in love and in whom God delights.

God created you for His own glory. What business, then, do you have trying to change yourself, to make yourself fit into some invisible standard that you don't even understand? You are created for the glory of God, made because God knows you, every part of you, inside and out, and He. Loves. You. All of you: the insecurities, the talents, the griefs, the joys, the mediocre. At the darkest bends in your life and at your most triumphant moments, God is with you, loving you, yearning to be with you, just as you are. You are perfect and you are beloved and you are worthy of God's love. You do not need to change.

It breaks my heart that there might be moments when this isn't a truth you really believe. If I only ever do one thing in my life, if my ministry only ever has one incarnation, I hope that it will be this: that I kept my baptismal promise, that I will be a constant, persistent, always true voice proclaiming the joyful reality of your preciousness to you, always finding Christ in you and showing you that grace. When voices are pressuring you to change, to conform, to mold yourself to some ideal of what is "right" and "good" and "holy," I want to always be on the other side reminding you that you, you right there right now, you are right and good and holy just as you are. I want to tattoo the word "beloved" on the tender skin over your heart so that you feel it there with each rush of blood through your veins. I want to stamp it across your forehead so that when the sure steady beat of your heart is not quite enough to convince you, a single look in the mirror each day will remind you that you are perfect and loved eternally, for always, forever. And if that is not enough, if you need more proof, I want you to know this: that you are a blessing in my life, that you fill me with joy, that you are wonderful and precious to me, and that I thank God every day for the service He did when He walked you into my world.

You are loved.

You are precious.

You are perfect.

Let it wash over you. Say it over and over again until it becomes second-nature. Let yourself see it in the world around you, in the miracle of creation, in every person you love. Start seeking God's grace in the world and serving Him by sharing this message with everyone you know. Open up your ears, because bit by bit as this miraculous truth winds its way into your heart, you will begin to hear God's voice, calling out to you as it always has been and always will be:

"Do not fear, for I have redeemed you. I have called you by name, and you are mine . . . For I am the Lord your God, the Holy One of Israel, your Savior. I give Egypt as your ransom, Ethiopia and Seba in exchange for you. Because you are precious in my sight, and honored, and I love you, I give people in return for you, nations in exchange for your life" (Isaiah 43:1, 3–4).

Cate Anthony, Christ Church Christiana Hundred,
Greenville, Delaware

I'm a junior in high school and a baptized child of God. I do not regularly attend church, nor do I regularly attend youth group meetings. But I am an instrument of God nonetheless.

I have built well houses for the less fortunate, dug trenches for those living in flood zones, and built houses for those who cannot afford professional contractors. I find Christ in other people—not in a service or the Eucharist. God calls us to love our neighbors as ourselves, and to spread the Good News of His loving kingdom through mission, teaching, and nurturing a community.

My passion is helping others, and until the day I can't drive a nail, I will build for God. Until I can't sing, I'll praise His great mercy. Until I die, I will follow Him.

Mitchell Abbott, Trinity Episcopal Church, Covington, Kentucky

Will you strive for justice and peace among all people and respect the dignity of every human being?

As I reflect on this simple promise that we all make when we say the Baptismal Covenant, I begin to think about all of the ways that I have lived out this promise throughout my ministry. And one of my favorites is joining our brothers and sisters at the BWI Airport where several of them are being paid unfair wages. Where is the justice? So as a leader at St. Philip's Episcopal Church, I invited a worker to speak at St. Philip's to share his story about the injustice at the airport. I have also decided to join Maryland's Interfaith Worker Justice (IWJ) to encourage other workers to unleash their voices. God has called all of us to strive for justice and peace among all people and IWJ has given me the platform to do so!

Randy Callender, St. Philip's Episcopal Church, Annapolis, Maryland

Prayers & Voices

We thank you, Almighty God, for the gift of water. Over it the Holy Spirit moved in the beginning of creation. Through it you led the children of Israel out of their bondage in Egypt into the land of promise. In it your Son Jesus received the baptism of John and was anointed by the Holy Spirit as the Messiah, the Christ, to lead us, through his death and resurrection, from the bondage of sin into everlasting life.

We thank you, Father, for the water of Baptism. In it we are buried with Christ in his death. By it we share in his resurrection. Through it we are reborn by the Holy Spirit. Therefore in joyful obedience to your Son, we bring into his fellowship those who come to him in faith, baptizing them in the Name of the Father, and of the Son, and of the Holy Spirit.

Now sanctify this water, we pray you, by the power of your Holy Spirit, that those who here are cleansed from sin and born again may continue for ever in the risen life of Jesus Christ our Savior.

To him, to you, and to the Holy Spirit, be all honor and glory, now and for ever. Amen.

The Prayer over Water at Holy Baptism, BCP, pp. 306–307

Almighty God, we thank you that by the death and resurrection of your Son Jesus Christ you have overcome sin and brought us to yourself, and that by the sealing of your Holy Spirit you have bound us to your service. Renew in these your servants the covenant you made with them at their Baptism. Send them forth in the power of that Spirit to perform the service you set before them; through Jesus Christ your Son our Lord, who lives and reigns with you and the Holy Spirit, one God, now and for ever. Amen.

At Confirmation, Reception, or Reaffirmation, BCP, p. 309 or 418

"I always knew that deep down in every human heart, there was mercy and generosity. No one is born hating another person because of the colour of his skin, or his background, or his religion. People must learn to hate, and if they can learn to hate, they can be taught to love, for love comes more naturally to the human heart than its opposite. Even in the grimmest times in prison, when my comrades and I were pushed to our limits, I would see a glimmer of humanity in one of the guards, perhaps just for a second, but it was enough to reassure me and keep me going. Man's goodness is a flame that can be hidden but never extinguished."

Nelson Mandela (1918–2013), former President of South Africa, 1993 Nobel Peace Prize recipient

Almighty God, look with favor upon us who have reaffirmed our commitment to follow Christ and to serve in his name. Give us courage, patience, and vision; and strengthen us all in our Christian vocation of witness to the world, and of service to others; through Jesus Christ our Lord. Amen.

For Reaffirmation (adapted), BCP, p. 421

"Preach the Gospel at all times, and when necessary, use words."

St. Francis of Assisi (1181–1226), Italian Catholic Friar

"You never go away from us, yet we have difficulty in returning to You. Come, Lord, stir us up and call us back. Kindle and seize us. Be our fire and our sweetness. Let us love. Let us run."

Augustine of Hippo (354–430),
early Christian theologian from North Africa

Holy Spirit, you join us together in a common bond of love and faith in Jesus Christ. Keep all churches focused on God's mission of healing and reconciliation of all people. Give wisdom to those who lead the church: lay leaders, deacons, priests, and bishops. Strengthen all of us to do your work in the world, so that we will be drawn closer to your kingdom here on earth and every day. Amen.

From "Call on Me: A Prayer Book for Young People," p. 17

O God, whose blessed Son made himself known to his disciples in the breaking of the bread: Open the eyes of our faith, that we may behold him in all his redeeming work; who lives and reigns with you, in the unity of the Holy Spirit, one God, now and forever. Amen.

Collect for the Third Sunday of Easter, BCP, p. 224

Dieu tout-puissant, nous te rendons grâce, car par la mort et la resurrection de ton Fils, tu as vaincu le péché et tu nous as ramenés vers toi: par le sceau de l'Esprit Saint tu nous attachés à ton service. Renouvellen tes serviteurs, ici presents, l'Alliance que tu as conclude avec eux à leur baptême. Envoie-les mainte-

nant accomplir, dans la puissance de l'Espirt le service auquel tu
les destines. Par Jésus Christ, ton Fils, notre Seigneur, qui vit et
règne avec toi, en l'unité due Saint-Esprit, un seul Dieu, mainte-
nant et toujours. Amen.

A la confirmation, l'admission dans la communion de l'Eglise,
ou le renouvellement des promesses du Baptême, BCP, p. 217

"Prayer is not asking. It is a longing of the soul. It is daily admission of one's weakness. It is better in prayer to have a heart
without words than words without a heart."

Mohandas Karamchand Gandhi (1869–1948),
Hindu leader of India who practiced non-violent civil disobedience

Gracious God, in baptism you make us one family in Christ your
Son, one in the sharing of his body and blood, one in the communion of his Spirit. Help us to grow in love for one another
and come to the full maturity of the body of Christ. Most loving
God, you send us into the world you love. Give us grace to go
thankfully and with courage in the power of your Spirit.

From "Two Thousand Years of Prayer," p. 508

Father in heaven, who at the baptism of Jesus in the River
Jordan proclaimed him your beloved Son and anointed him with
the Holy Spirit: Grant that all who are baptized into his Name
may keep the covenant they have made, and boldly confess him
as Lord and Savior; who with you and the Holy Spirit lives and
reigns, one God, in glory everlasting. Amen.

Collect for The Baptism of our Lord, BCP, p. 214

"To worship is to quicken the conscience by the holiness of God, to feed the mind with the truth of God, to purge the imagination by the beauty of God, to open the heart to the love of God, to devote the will to the purpose of God."

William Temple (1881–1944), Archbishop of Canterbury 1942–44

". . . we are to be lights in the world. It is God's business to light us, to set us on the lampstand, and to bring the people into the house. Our only duty is to shine forth with the gospel."

Marva J. Dawn (1948–), American theologian

Oh Dios, por medio de la enseñanza du tu Hijo Jesucristo preparaste a tus discípulos para la venida del Espíritu Santo: Haz que los corazones y las mentes de tus siervos estén listos par recibir la bendición del Espíritu Santo, a fin de que sean llenos del poder de su presencia; por Jesucristo nuestro Señor. Amén.

Por los que van a ser bautizados o los que van a renovar su Pacto Bautismal, Oraciones, BCP, p. 709

The Simple Path
Silence is Prayer
Prayer is Faith
Faith is Love
Love is Service
The Fruit of Service is Peace

Mother Teresa of Calcutta (1910–1997),
1979 Nobel Peace Prize recipient

Almighty God, who created us in your own image: Grant us grace fearlessly to contend against evil and to make no peace with oppression; and, that we may reverently use our freedom, help us to employ it in the maintenance of justice in our communities and among the nations, so the glory of your holy Name; through Jesus Christ our Lord, who lives and reigns with you and the Holy Spirit, one God, now and for ever. Amen.

For Social Justice, BCP, p. 260

Remember the Sabbath day, and keep it holy.

Exodus 20:8

Love the dispossessed, all those who, living amid human injustice, thirst after justice. Jesus had special concern for them. Have no fear of being disturbed by them.

From the "Rule of Taizé," an ecumenical monastic order in France

THE FIVE MARKS OF MISSION

O God, you have made of one blood all the peoples of the earth, and sent your blessed Son to preach peace to those who are far off and to those who are near: Grant that people everywhere may seek after you and find you, bring the nations into your fold, pour out your Spirit upon all flesh, and hasten the coming of your kingdom; through Jesus Christ our Lord, who lives and reigns with you and the Holy Spirit, one God, now and for ever. Amen.

For the Mission of the Church, BCP, p. 257

The Five Marks of Mission

The Mission of the Church Is the Mission of Christ
1. To proclaim the Good News of the Kingdom
2. To teach, baptize, and nurture new believers
3. To respond to human need by loving service
4. To seek to transform unjust structures of society, to challenge violence of every kind, and to pursue peace and reconciliation
5. To strive to safeguard the integrity of creation and sustain and renew the life of the earth

La mission de l'Église est ell du Christ
1. Proclamer la Bonne Nouvelle du Royaume de Dieu
2. Instruire, baptizer, et encourager les nouveaux croyants
3. Répondre par amour aux besoins humains
4. S'efforcer de transformer toutes structures injustes de la société, confronter toutes violences, et rechercher la paix et lat reconciliation
5. Œuvrer pour la sauvegarde de l'intégrité de la creation et soutenir et renouveler la vie de la terre

La mission de la Iglesia es la mission de Cristo
1. Proclamar las Buenas Nuevas del Reino
2. Enseñar, bautizar, y nutrir a lost neuvos creyentes
3. Responder a la necesidad humana mediante un servicio de amor
4. Tratar de transformer las estructuras injustas de la sociedad, enfrentar la violencia de toda indole, y buscar la paz y la reconcilación
5. Luchar por salvaguardar la integridad del la creación y sostener y renovar la vida en la tierra

Mission and Ministry

God's Mission is our mission. We are called to partner with one another to restore all people to unity with God and each other in Christ. We do this by prayer and worshipping together, by proclaiming the Gospel, and promoting justice, peace, and love in our daily life—at work, at home, at school, and in our communities—through the various ministries God calls us.

All of us are ministers in God's Church, whether we are lay persons, bishops, priests, or deacons. Each of us has a ministry to represent Christ by bearing witness to Christ wherever we may be according to the gifts we are given by God. This may be through speaking up when we see an injustice, praying for someone, serving a person or agency in need, or listening to a friend. There are countless ways each of us can share in helping heal the world. As Christians we are to share our relationships in the mission of God to the wider world, bearing witness to the kingdom of love, justice, and joy that Jesus began. Whatever we do to carry on Christ's work of reconciliation and restoration of hope and peace with those we encounter helps God's mission.

As Christians we are called to join God's mission. As the Christian Church, we are called to serve in mission in communion with all the saints. But, discerning our particular personal and communal role in engaging God's mission can feel overwhelming, unclear, or even confusing.

So, how do we get started on such a monumental task? Perhaps it is most helpful to begin with prayerful thought about WHO God is calling you to become through a mission opportunity: a companion, witness, pilgrim, servant, prophet, ambassador, host, or sacrament?

A Companion

God is calling our church, as a whole, to be a companion with other churches and beyond. Dioceses and congregations are living out their calling to become companions with dioceses and congregations in our country and around the world. Individual missionaries are ministering as companions in the places where they are called to serve. Literally, companions share bread together.

Now when Jesus heard this, he withdrew from there in a boat to a deserted place by himself. But when the crowds heard it, they followed him on foot from the towns. When he went ashore, he saw a great crowd; and he had compassion for them and cured their sick. When it was evening, the disciples came to him and said, "This is a deserted place, and the hour is now late; send the crowds away so that they may go into the villages and buy food for themselves." Jesus said to them, "They need not go away; you give them something to eat." They replied, "We have nothing here but five loaves and two fish." And he said, "Bring them here to me." Then he ordered the crowds to sit down on the grass. Taking the five loaves and the two fish, he looked up to heaven, and blessed and broke the loaves, and gave them to the disciples, and the disciples gave them to the crowds. And all ate and were filled; and they took up what was left over of the broken pieces, twelve baskets full. And those who ate were about five thousand men, besides women and children. (Matthew 14:13–21)

A Witness

"You are witnesses of these things," said Jesus to his disciples.
Witness is a word that means sharing the story of what God
has done with us, in light of the story of what God has done in
Christ Jesus. Such witnessing is the natural and inevitable fruit
of a life in Christ, and it is the heart of evangelism as a mission
imperative.

*Now when Jesus learned that the Pharisees had heard, "Jesus is
making and baptizing more disciples than John"—although it was not
Jesus himself but his disciples who baptized—he left Judea and started
back to Galilee. But he had to go through Samaria. So he came to a
Samaritan city called Sychar, near the plot of ground that Jacob had
given to his son Joseph. Jacob's well was there, and Jesus, tired out by
his journey, was sitting by the well. It was about noon.*

    *A Samaritan woman came to draw water, and Jesus said to her,
"Give me a drink." (His disciples had gone to the city to buy food.)
The Samaritan woman said to him, "How is it that you, a Jew, ask a
drink of me, a woman of Samaria?" (Jews do not share things in common with Samaritans.) Jesus answered her, "If you knew the gift of
God, and who it is that is saying to you, 'Give me a drink,' you would
have asked him, and he would have given you living water." The
woman said to him, "Sir, you have no bucket, and the well is deep.
Where do you get that living water? Are you greater than our ancestor
Jacob, who gave us the well, and with his sons and his flocks drank
from it?" Jesus said to her, "Everyone who drinks of this water will be
thirsty again, but those who drink of the water that I will give them will
never be thirsty. The water that I will give will become in them a spring
of water gushing up to eternal life." The woman said to him, "Sir, give*

me this water, so that I may never be thirsty or have to keep coming here to draw water." . . . Then the woman left her water jar and went back to the city. She said to the people, "Come and see a man who told me everything I have ever done! He cannot be the Messiah, can he?" They left the city and were on their way to him. . . .

Many Samaritans from that city believed in him because of the woman's testimony, "He told me everything I have ever done." So when the Samaritans came to him, they asked him to stay with them; and he stayed there for two days. And many more believed because of his word. They said to the woman, "It is no longer because of what you said that we believe, for we have heard for ourselves, and we know that this is truly the Savior of the world." (John 4:1–15, 28–30, 39–42)

A Pilgrim

Episcopal missionaries today see themselves as pilgrims, growing in their knowledge of God through the perspectives of the people to whom they are sent, learning as much as they share, receiving as much as they give.

All of these died in faith without having received the promises, but from a distance they saw and greeted them. They confessed that they were strangers and foreigners on the earth, for people who speak in this way make it clear that they are seeking a homeland. If they had been thinking of the land that they had left behind, they would have had opportunity to return. But as it is, they desire a better country, that is, a heavenly one. Therefore God is not ashamed to be called their God; indeed, he has prepared a city for them. (Hebrews 11:13–16)

A Servant

"I came not to be served but to serve," said Jesus. Servant-hood in mission means that we listen to the stated needs of our mission companions, look for signs of God's work in them, and collaborate with them in discerning how God is guiding the implementation of mission vision. It means that missionaries and the church put aside prior images of our companions, pre-conceived analyses of their situations, and ready-made solutions to their problems.

If then there is any encouragement in Christ, any consolation from love, any sharing in the Spirit, any compassion and sympathy, make my joy complete: be of the same mind, having the same love, being in full accord and of one mind. Do nothing from selfish ambition or conceit, but in humility regard others as better than yourselves. Let each of you look not to your own interests, but to the interests of others. Let the same mind be in you that was in Christ Jesus, who, though he was in the form of God, did not regard equality with God as something to be exploited, but emptied himself, taking the form of a slave, being born in human likeness. And being found in human form, he humbled himself and became obedient to the point of death—even death on a cross.

Therefore God also highly exalted him and gave him the name that is above every name, so that at the name of Jesus every knee should bend, in heaven and on earth and under the earth, and every tongue should confess that Jesus Christ is Lord, to the glory of God the Father. (Philippians 2:1–11)

A Prophet

Episcopal mission pilgrims today often find their views of political, racial, and economic relationships in the world challenged and transformed. Experiences of poverty, suffering, and violence alongside experiences of affluence, oppression, and security often radicalize missionaries, whether they are long-term missioners, visiting bishops, or short-term teams. These are prophesy to the sending church, prodding it to inquire more deeply into dynamics about which it may have become complacent or resigned.

The spirit of the Lord God is upon me,
    because the Lord has anointed me;
he has sent me to bring good news to the oppressed,
    to bind up the brokenhearted,
to proclaim liberty to the captives,
    and release to the prisoners;
to proclaim the year of the Lord's favor,
    and the day of vengeance of our God;
    to comfort all who mourn;
to provide for those who mourn in Zion—
    to give them a garland instead of ashes,
the oil of gladness instead of mourning,
    the mantle of praise instead of a faint spirit.
They will be called oaks of righteousness,
    the planting of the Lord, to display his glory.
They shall build up the ancient ruins,
    they shall raise up the former devastations;
they shall repair the ruined cities,
    the devastations of many generations.

(Isaiah 61:1–4)

An Ambassador

In addition to witness in word and deed as ambassadors of Christ, the missionary and missionary communities are ambassadors of the sending church. This calls for living out the highest ethical standards in personal honesty, respect for others, financial transparency, and faithfulness in personal and professional relationships.

If you put these instructions before the brothers and sisters, you will be a good servant of Christ Jesus, nourished on the words of the faith and of the sound teaching that you have followed. Have nothing to do with profane myths and old wives' tales. Train yourself in godliness, for, while physical training is of some value, godliness is valuable in every way, holding promise for both the present life and the life to come. The saying is sure and worthy of full acceptance. For to this end we toil and struggle, because we have our hope set on the living God, who is the Savior of all people, especially of those who believe.

These are the things you must insist on and teach. Let no one despise your youth, but set the believers an example in speech and conduct, in love, in faith, in purity. Until I arrive, give attention to the public reading of scripture, to exhorting, to teaching. Do not neglect the gift that is in you, which was given to you through prophecy with the laying on of hands by the council of elders. Put these things into practice, devote yourself to them, so that all may see your progress. Pay close attention to yourself and to your teaching; continue in these things, for in doing this you will save both yourself and your hearers.
(1 Timothy 4:6–16)

A Host

"Let a little water be brought, and wash your feet," said Abraham to the three strangers who appeared at Mamre. "Let it be to me according to your word," said Mary to the angel Gabriel. In initiating mission, God does not force us, but invites a response of hospitality.

Now as they went on their way, he entered a certain village, where a woman named Martha welcomed him into her home. She had a sister named Mary, who sat at the Lord's feet and listened to what he was saying. But Martha was distracted by her many tasks; so she came to him and asked, "Lord, do you not care that my sister has left me to do all the work by myself? Tell her then to help me." But the Lord answered her, "Martha, Martha, you are worried and distracted by many things; there is need of only one thing. Mary has chosen the better part, which will not be taken away from her." (Luke 10:38–42)

Now a certain man was ill, Lazarus of Bethany, the village of Mary and her sister Martha. Mary was the one who anointed the Lord with perfume and wiped his feet with her hair; her brother Lazarus was ill. So the sisters sent a message to Jesus, "Lord, he whom you love is ill." But when Jesus heard it, he said, "This illness does not lead to death; rather it is for God's glory, so that the Son of God may be glorified through it." Accordingly, though Jesus loved Martha and her sister and Lazarus, after having heard that Lazarus was ill, he stayed two days longer in the place where he was.

Then after this he said to the disciples, "Let us go to Judea again." The disciples said to him, "Rabbi, the Jews were just now trying to stone you, and are you going there again?" Jesus answered,

"Are there not twelve hours of daylight? Those who walk during the day do not stumble, because they see the light of this world. But those who walk at night stumble, because the light is not in them." After saying this, he told them, "Our friend Lazarus has fallen asleep, but I am going there to awaken him." The disciples said to him, "Lord, if he has fallen asleep, he will be all right." (John 11:1–12)

A Sacrament

As the body of Christ, the church is a sacrament of Christ, an outward and visible sign of Christ's inward and spiritual grace. As members of the body, all Christians participate in the communion of the saints and so are members of the sacramental revelation of God, embodied in the incarnation of Jesus Christ. A Christian on mission is a sacramental sign of God's mission to reconcile all people with one another and God in Christ.

Now on that same day two of them were going to a village called Emmaus, about seven miles from Jerusalem, and talking with each other about all these things that had happened. While they were talking and discussing, Jesus himself came near and went with them, but their eyes were kept from recognizing him. And he said to them, "What are you discussing with each other while you walk along?" They stood still, looking sad. Then one of them, whose name was Cleopas, answered him, "Are you the only stranger in Jerusalem who does not know the things that have taken place there in these days?" He asked them, "What things?" They replied, "The things about Jesus of Nazareth, who was a prophet mighty in deed and word before God and all the people, and how our chief priests and leaders handed him over to be condemned to death and crucified him. But we had hoped that he was the one to redeem Israel. Yes, and besides all this, it is now the third day since these things took place. Moreover, some women of our group astounded us. They were at the tomb early this morning, and when they did not find his body there, they came back and told us that they had indeed seen a vision of angels who said that he was alive. Some of those who were with us went to the tomb and found it just as the women had said; but they did not see him." Then he said to them, "Oh, how foolish you are, and how slow of heart to believe all that the prophets have declared! Was it not necessary that the Messiah should suffer these things and then enter into his glory?" Then beginning with Moses and all the prophets, he interpreted to them the things about himself in all the scriptures.

As they came near the village to which they were going, he walked ahead as if he were going on. But they urged him strongly, saying, "Stay with us, because it is almost evening and the day is now nearly over." So he went in to stay with them. When he was at the table with them, he took bread, blessed and broke it, and gave it to them. Then their eyes were opened, and they recognized him; and he vanished from their sight. They said to each other, "Were not our hearts burning within us while he was talking to us on the road, while he was opening the scriptures to us?" That same hour they got up and returned to Jerusalem; and they found the eleven and their companions gathered together. They were saying, "The Lord has risen indeed, and he has appeared to Simon!" Then they told what had happened on the road, and how he had been made known to them in the breaking of the bread. (Luke 24:13–35)

> *Excerpt from the "Episcopal Youth in Mission Manual,"*
> *by Cookie Cantwell (Diocese of East Carolina),*
> *Beth Crow (Diocese of North Carolina),*
> *and Wendy Johnson (Diocese of Minnesota).*

The Five Marks of Mission, in addition to our Baptismal Promises, can help us focus on how to live out God's mission. Developed by the Anglican Consultative Council in 1984 and 1990, and adopted by The Episcopal Church's General Convention in 2009, the Five Marks are a way for us to recognize our common call to share in God's healing and reconciling mission for our blessed but broken and hurting world.

All mission is done in a particular setting—the context. While we are united in the Good News of Christ, we each come from a diversity of places, times, and cultures in which we live, proclaim, and embody God's Mission. Worship is central to our life as Christians together, and as Episcopalians each time we celebrate the Eucharist, we proclaim Christ's death until he comes again. Holy bread and wine feeds us to do the work God has given us to do.

The first mark of mission is really a summary of what all mission is about because it is based on Jesus' own summary of his mission—announcing the Good News. When Jesus began his ministry after his baptism, he began to proclaim, "Repent, for the kingdom of heaven has come near" (Matthew 4:17). Luke 4:18–19 describes Jesus quoting from the scroll of the prophet Isaiah in the synagogue in Nazareth, "The Spirit of the Lord is upon me, because he has anointed me to bring good news to the poor. He has sent me to proclaim release to the captives and recovery of sight to the blind, to let the oppressed go free, to proclaim the year of the Lord's favor."

The Five Marks stress the doing of mission. The challenge is not just to do mission, but also to be a people of mission. Each Mark offers a framework for mission and ministry work. This may already be part of your church's mission work or personal ministry. Whether it's when you recycle (Mark #5), undertake social justice work (Mark #4), donate to a food pantry or volunteer at a soup kitchen (Mark #3), renew your baptismal vows (Marks #1 and #2), or in any other way, the Five Marks of Mission shine through.

In Action

Mark #1: To proclaim the Good News of the Kingdom

Proclamation needs to be not only in words — effective communication of the Gospel — but also in actions, by living the Good News we preach.

One of my experiences with the Marks of Mission is to proclaim the Good News of the Lord to those who have no resources to go to a church and those who have a disability. I daily proclaim that God is good all the time. I also teach children and young people of my generation because we're the vision of the future world. I look for new believers and encourage them to follow Christ, praying that every act of injustice, discrimination, violence, or racism toward them is removed, believing in God to keep us together forever.

Rosanna Vizcaino, La transfiguracion Bani,
Provincia Peravia, Republica Dominicana

On my college campus, there is no traditional Episcopal Campus Ministry to proclaim the Good News of the Kingdom. So I go to the local church in the town where my college sits. I never really invited anyone to church with me before I came to college — but I did not want to go alone. First, I invited my roommate, then a girl who lives across from my hall. By the time fall break came along, I had brought four or five other people to church who would not have gone to a church on their own. I live out the Five Marks of Mission by bringing others along with me to church — because sometimes all it takes is a little push to start someone on their own faith journey.

Ben Cowgill, St. Timothy's, Winston-Salem, North Carolina

One amazing experience I had was when I sung the song, "Imagine" by John Lennon at Holy Family Episcopal Church during a family reunion. I saw how the words and my emotions touched everyone during my performance. Many were witnesses of the deep message in that song.

Tonie Renaud, Church of the Resurrection, Miami, Florida

Mark #2: To teach, baptize, and nurture new believers

Christian discipleship is about lifelong learning. We all need formal and informal resources for growing in faith, so that the church is a learning environment for all ages.

As a member of the EYE Mission Planning team, we chose to have the 5 Marks of Mission as the theme for EYE 2014. I believe that EYE can integrate all 5 Marks of Mission, and it wouldn't be the same if all 5 Marks were not present. However, the first two Marks are what I think both EYE and youth ministries at every level strive to live out. Whether it is a huge, international event for a thousand people, or a small parish's five-person "youth group" (such as my own), youth ministry is all about proclaiming the Good News of the kingdom, and teaching, baptizing, and nurturing believers.

Kayden Nasworthy, St. Andrew's Episcopal Church,
Ayer, Massachusetts

I am a verger in my home parish, which is a layperson that assists the Rector in the preparing and conducting of worship services. This is a very broad definition for a very broad ministry, but one of my favorite parts is working with the acolytes.

In recent months, our parish has had a huge increase in the amount of fourth and fifth graders. Meaning, we have lots of new acolytes! So, I have had the joy of training these new acolytes. Some of the trainings have been wonderful and productive; some have been stressful and overwhelming. However, every time I walk away from the church after training an acolyte, I feel like God is smiling down on our church. There our young people are getting the chance to experience our beautiful liturgy in fun ways. The vestments and processions enchant most of the kids as if they are experiencing something God-like. That's because they are! I am honored to serve the Church as a teacher, bringing these young, creative, and energetic people closer into the loving embrace of God.

Thomas Alexander, St. Margaret's Episcopal Church,
Little Rock, Arkansas

As a godmother of four young people, and the fairy godmother of one young woman, I think about appropriate ways to teach and nurture these humans. I was present at most of their baptisms and made promises to "be responsible for seeing that the child you present is brought up in the Christian faith and life." Discerning how to do that, especially with those goddaughters who live a great distance away, has been an interesting challenge.

Clearly I need to be in active relationship with all of these godchildren and I have discerned that praying for them regularly and intentionally is an important strategy in fulfilling my promise. I travel extensively for work and my prayer discipline has also become a ministry of sending old-fashioned postcards not only to my godchildren, but also to my sons, nieces, and nephews, and other assorted children in my life.

While visiting my twin nine-year-old goddaughters in Florida last spring, they were eager to show me all of the treasures they keep on a special shelf in their room. When we finished with that portion of the show-and-tell, they hauled out a photo album and I was shocked and delighted to discover it was full of all the postcards I have mailed to them to date. I had falsely assumed that they would be posted to the refrigerator for a few weeks and then be discarded to the recycling bin once they had fallen to the floor a few too many times. Karen and Grace love getting postcards from me, and they send me an occasional postcard, too. This practice of connectivity helps me to maintain a unique and loving relationship with them so that we feel as though we share something personal and special when we get to meet in person.

My oldest goddaughter, Maria, still lives in our hometown. She, too, has saved all of her postcards from me and plans to preserve them so that she can read them when she's feeling lonely or can't find a way to pray. She says that they remind her that I love her and I am always thinking of her and praying for her. When she has questions about Christianity, The Episcopal Church, or about her own life and discernment, she knows she can pray about them and that she can always get in touch with me for a conversation.

I never dreamed that a ministry of postcards would be a spiritual practice of prayer and nurture. But it fits and it provides common ground for future conversations. How might you engage this mark of mission to teach, baptize, and nurture new believers?

Bronwyn Clark Skov, Hastings, Minnesota

Mark #3: To respond to human need by loving service

Churches have a long tradition of care through pastoral and social ministry. Christians are called to respond to the needs of people locally and in the wider human community.

Like most recent college graduates, I spent some time working in the service industry. I always thought of myself as a people person, and my job required that I work with or around people for my whole day. After three years, I decided maybe I wasn't as much of one as I had thought. But after spending time working with people in Baltimore, where they saw me as an equal or as a mentor figure, I found that it wasn't that I didn't like people, I just did not want to be treated like a subhuman.

Many people see a person in the service industry as someone who loves to be of service. This may vary from waitress to barista, but I really do love helping people. Turns out that I was a favorite staff member because I would always be genuine with my "Good morning, how are you?" I love people, helping, and being of service to others. Turns out that it is just in a more complex way than I had imagined. Working for the youth ministry office is the most rewarding thing I could ever imagine.

Kate Riley, Emmanuel Episcopal Church, Cumberland, Maryland

This summer I was lucky enough to be able to volunteer at my diocesan camp, Grace Point. Every year Grace Point has a few outreach camps, including one called Camp Billy Johnson. This is a camp for very poor children, including some who are homeless. This particular week of the summer was probably the greatest of my life. Although I did feel as if I was responding to human need by loving service, these kids were helping me more than I could have ever helped them. They were the happiest and most grateful people I have ever met. They taught me to enjoy and acknowledge the little joys of life. From this experience I learned that even though I may try to live out a Mark of Mission, I may get more from it than I actually give.

Rebecca Brewer, St. Paul's Episcopal Church, Kingsport, Tennessee

The week that our youth group spent in Skid Row, Los Angeles, was one of the most life-changing experiences I've ever had as an Episcopalian. "To respond to human need through loving service" is something that I learned we all could do. Whether it was serving meals in a soup kitchen, playing soccer with kids in a low-income housing project, or sharing pastries with the homeless in Pershing Square, I learned that the littlest things could have the biggest impact on others. There is truly no feeling like putting a smile on someone's face, especially at the small price of a donut or a few hours of your time. I also learned an important distinction between plain old service and "loving" service. Doing things with the spirit in your heart and a smile on your face truly does make a difference, and that difference is apparent to others. Doing good deeds is great, but doing it in a way that reflects the most important Christian value — love — is what makes a good deed meaningful.

Casey Nakamura, All Saints Church, Kapaa, Hawaii

Last summer a number of churches went to a small town in Alabama to help with tornado relief. The town had been hit by a number of tornados that decimated the area. The only thing standing was a bank vault. The girls spent the time working on a police station, painting the inside and out, cleaning, and decorating. The officers often visited them to thank them. The boys were taken to an empty lot that had once seen someone's house. It was covered in trash, weeds, and old memories. We set to working marking the boundaries of the lot and clearing it out. During this time a man drove up and thanked us for doing something he had been asking help with for a year.

That trip, and the service that occurred, has always struck out to me as the example for responding to others, and it has been inspiration for me to increase my level of service in every aspect of my life, both with my church and in the community.

Henry Jones, St. Martin's Episcopal Church,
Charlotte, North Carolina

A good portion of my life has revolved around Mark #3, to respond to human need by loving service. When I was thirteen, I spent three weeks of my summer living with my grandparents in Las Cruces, New Mexico, as sort of a "coming of age" vacation. That was definitely culture shock for a Nebraska boy — dry heat, no cows in sight, and I didn't take too well to my grandmother shoving V8 Juice down my throat because she was insistent that I hadn't eaten enough vegetables.

During my stay, my uncle was spearheading a fundraiser for a non-profit organization called Free Wheelchair Mission. Naturally, since I was an able-bodied teenager, I was roped into handling the dirty work — moving tables and wheelchairs, running around, and handling the meager little tasks that everybody else was avoiding with a purpose. Following a long day of being the event's water boy, I realized that I didn't even know what the whole thing was about. So, being the inquiring kid that I was, I sat down with my uncle and asked him what all the hoopla was about. Long story short, in 1976, an extremely successful bio-medical engineer was on vacation with his wife in Malaysia. The two witnessed a lame woman dragging herself across a dirt road in order to retrieve water for herself and her family. This image burned in the memory of the doctor, and he thus dropped his entire career in order to create a means to help the one hundred million physically incapacitated people in third-world countries. The chair he created cost less than $50, including shipping. I was absolutely mesmerized. At that moment, I felt a tug — a deep, knowing sensation that I needed to take this opportunity and run with it.

Two weeks following my return home, I pulled some strings and held my own fundraiser at my home church. One thing led to another, and soon I was traveling to churches, schools, and civic organizations statewide, tirelessly spreading the news of this wonderful organization. I spoke at numerous churches in the diocese and even spoke at three Annual Councils. From there, it all only got bigger. Elementary schools and youth groups used it as a service project, and I even got to meet the head of the organization himself in Los Angeles.

The Nebraska Youth for Locomotion campaign has raised almost $25,000 to date, a staggering number that I can barely grasp. Who knew that it was so simple to change a life — let alone five hundred lives? All it takes is one less night out to eat and a little bit of drive. There are 100,000,000 people in third-world countries in this world who cannot move on their own, and if we all live by the third mark a little bit more, who knows what this world could see.

Joe Prickett, St. Stephen's Episcopal Church, Grand Island, Nebraska

The Five Marks of Mission are an excellent set of guidelines by which to conduct our everyday lives. However, they may seem a little overwhelming when looked at as a whole. One specific Mark of Mission that I like to focus on is to respond to human need by loving service. This could be taken to mean something large, like helping to feed the homeless, but it also could just be listening to a friend who is going through hard times.

My best friend is going through some tough times these days, and one of the most valuable things I did to help her through was to surprise her with her favorite Starbucks drink one night. We sat on the porch, talked, and drank coffee for many hours. There were tears, laughter, and thoughtful silences. In the end, I was able to make her feel better, if only for a little while, by giving her an escape from hectic daily drama. Responding to human need isn't necessarily as big of a task as it sounds. We all have the power to make someone's day a little better.

Madeline Carroll, All Saints Episcopal Church,
Wauwatosa, Wisconsin

Mark #4: To seek to transform unjust structures of society, to challenge violence of every kind, and to pursue peace and reconciliation

Jesus, and the Old Testament prophets before him, challenged oppressive structures in God's name. Christians are called not only to press for change, but also to demonstrate justice within church structures.

I tried to transform unjust structures by advocating for resolution D067-2012 (The Dream Act) at the Episcopal General Convention. This would allow undocumented students and young adults that would like to strive for higher education attend college in a country that does not accept them and yet it is the one they are at home in. The House of Deputies affirmed this resolution by unanimous adoption.

Ariana Gonzalez-Bonillas, St. Matthew's Episcopal Church,
Chandler, Arizona

I believe that in the past six months or so, I have truly lived out the mark "To seek to transform unjust structures of society, to challenge violence of every kind, and to pursue peace and reconciliation." Throughout my whole life, my sisters and I were very afraid of someone we were very close to. This person would act out, and was very unpredictable with an ever-changing mood. I don't believe that any person should have to live in fear of another; I believe it is very unjust and it is most definitely a present issue in today's society.

In 2013, my mom and this person got into an argument and for the first time, my mom finally spoke up for herself and let him know that his actions were not going to be tolerated any more. Using my mom as a model, when I saw this person next, I realized I had to have an honest and up-front conversation with him. I let him know that because of his actions, I have lived in constant fear of him. Since this day, I have not seen him and I have only spoken to him through a text message.

I hope one day to be able to pursue reconciliation and maybe even salvage the relationship so we can celebrate holidays and birthdays together. As far as peace goes, with this kind of situation, it has to come from within. I think slowly we will all come to peace with what has happened and be able to recover and move on and learn from this.

Cydney Jackson, St. Bartholomew's Episcopal Church,
Poway, California

Last summer I had the opportunity to travel to Oświęcim, Poland to visit the infamous Auschwitz Concentration Camp.

The main gate at the entrance to Auschwitz proclaims, "Arbeit macht frei," which in English means, "Work makes you free." This was a trick perpetuated by the Nazis on the prisoners. It was meant to calm the masses entering the Camp by convincing them they had hope for survival if they just worked hard enough.

Like the prisoners of seventy-five years ago, I walked through those gates into Auschwitz. And from that point forward I was thrust into the single most transformative experience of my life.

Auschwitz is an unrelenting, pounding, exhausting experience witnessing to the most horrific acts imaginable. You may think this all happened seventy-five years ago and visiting this site is more history than experience. No. At Auschwitz, every step, every word, every thought is swimming in a sea of pain and agony that is fresh and real. Block after block of human cruelty, retold in photos, letters, pictures, and victims' belongings. The remains of the gas chamber. Unspeakable grief.

Visiting Auschwitz must sound like an exercise in self-flagellation. However, having spent a week walking the grounds in conversation and prayer and having six months of space and time to consider all I experienced, I have come to believe that Auschwitz is an important place of pilgrimage for every Christian.

Here is why:

Traveling to Auschwitz is a pilgrimage of lamentation. It is a reminder of all the cruelty that humans have and are capable of inflicting on each other. A reminder of the despair we sometimes feel in our own lives. Standing at the execution wall, placing a rock next to one of the candles lit by a fellow traveler, I could almost feel pain pouring from the walls of the surrounding buildings. It is impossible to visit this place and not break down into a puddle of grief. In our stoic society, we don't often allow ourselves that kind of outpouring of any emotion. At Auschwitz, there's no way around it. And we learn about this primal grief; that it is important to our souls to express this emotion and to feel this deeply. How would our human experience be different if we allowed ourselves this depth of feeling for each other?

Traveling to Auschwitz is a pilgrimage of claiming personal responsibility for the well-being and safety of others. As I grappled with the sheer size of the Camp, I had to wonder how many people had to look away as innocent neighbors were stolen from their homes and carried in trains to this terrible place? How many times have I looked away when someone was mistreated or bullied? How many times have I failed to act when someone needed me?

Traveling to Auschwitz is a pilgrimage of searching for the deepest meaning of peace. There is no other place on earth where the effects of uncontrolled violence are more evident than at Auschwitz. In the Camp's newest exhibit, children's drawings from the walls of the bunks are painstakingly re-created. Among these pictures, a butterfly. A symbol of freedom and gentleness and rebirth. A symbol of delicacy and peace. A poignant and lasting reminder from a spirit long ago extinguished by violence, yet forever searing a message of hope and peace onto our hearts. How would we be different as a society if we all had to witness these atrocities? How much more important would peace become if we really had to witness the real devastation that can be caused by violence?

Finally, traveling to Auschwitz is a pilgrimage of examining forgiveness. I had the great fortune of visiting Auschwitz with survivor and Mengele Twin, Eva Kor. She has forgiven the doctors who experimented on her and she has forgiven the Nazis for imprisoning her and murdering her family. She speaks often about how she needed to forgive so that her heart could heal. As Christians, Jesus tells us we are called to forgive seventy times seven (Matthew 18:22). But are some acts unforgivable? What does it mean to truly forgive someone? Can we stand at Auschwitz and draw out a deeper understanding of what reconciliation means? Can we practice our own forgiveness of others?

Making a pilgrimage of this sort is setting aside time to really think about WHO we are called to be as Christians and WHO WE WANT TO BE when we are called to face situations of grief, violence, peacemaking, forgiveness, and personal responsibility.

Yes, this was a lot to consider in one seven-day period. However, I suspect the deeper reflections will come over time as I continue to untangle the various threads of this experience.

Wendy Johnson, All Saints Indian Mission, Minneapolis, Minnesota

Mark #5: To strive to safeguard the integrity of creation and sustain and renew the life of the earth

The Bible's vision of salvation is universal in its scope. We are called to promote the well-being of the human community and its environment, so that Creation may live in harmony.

Camp Washington, the Episcopal Diocese of Connecticut's camp and conference center, is an exemplary case of how the Marks of Missions are being fulfilled; none more than this fifth mark. The camp promotes the integrity of the environment on a daily basis. Campers measure their own "ort," which is wasted food, after every meal, and they learn to put on their plates only what they can eat. They also garden, maintain the trails, and learn about God's creation right in the midst of it.

The camp also safeguards the human community created between campers, staff, and the surrounding environment. The stresses of school and social status are broken as they come together and accomplish whatever it is they please, whether it is learning a new sport, dance, or even the seemingly simple task of communicating with one another. The 300-acre grounds provide somewhat of a social and educational paradise where they can feel free to learn, love, and even make the occasional mistake. Every camper leaves going back to their hometowns and schools bringing with them a piece of that integrity.

Chris Pearson, Camp Washington, Diocese of Connecticut

After graduating from college, I spent a year working in Malawi. I didn't make much money and resources were scarce, so my life became significantly simpler— fewer clothes, hardly any furniture, not much variety in food I ate. I didn't realize just how deeply this had affected me until I returned home. After nearly twenty-four hours of travel, I arrived in Chicago without any of my luggage: no clean clothes, no toothbrush, no deodorant.

My reintroduction to American culture began almost immediately with a trip to Target. My list was short. I only needed the basics. I got stuck on the deodorant, though. Sure, I found the deodorant aisle just fine, but that was the problem. There was a deodorant *aisle*. There I stood, staring at a wall covered in deodorant. Brand after brand, every one of them in a host of scents, some for sensitive skin, others with antiperspirant protections. The whole wall covered in different colors and patterns, neatly marked with price tags, speckled with little notices vying for my attention: buy one get one free, new low price, as advertised. Choice brought paralysis rather than freedom. In that moment, I longed for something simpler.

What are the things that clutter your life? What are the things that clamor for your attention and leave you feeling stuck? What might set you free? For me, Lent has become about seeking out simplicity, about reducing the number of inessential things clamoring for my attention. At times, this has meant choosing disciplines that limit my consumption. At other times, it has looked like carving out daily space for prayer or silence. I invite you to imagine what simplicity looks like in your life, to find one practice that will make your life more spacious. In doing so may you leave room to find and be found by God.

Phillip Fackler, Diocese of Chicago

Several years ago I led a lock-in at my church to explore the nature of global poverty with the youth from my parish. Our goal was to have a solidarity experience with those in the developing world and learn how we might fight against poverty. So we checked our cell phones at the door and, with our imaginations, transformed the parish hall into a village in the developing world. We limited ourselves to the resources that a teenager might have in a rural African village—which meant no electricity, limited food and water, and cramped sleeping locations.

We played educational games and prayed for our brothers and sisters. Perhaps the most impactful portion of the event had to do with clean water and sanitation. One of the most shocking realizations is that Americans use more clean, drinkable water in one flush of the toilet (on average five to seven gallons) than those in the Global South use in a whole day for cleaning, drinking, and washing. Sadly, the water in our toilets is often cleaner than the water that others are forced to drink. With that in mind, we instituted a policy for our bathroom usage: "If it's yellow, let it mellow and if it's brown, flush it down." The teens were hesitant at first, but embraced the concept when they remembered those in the developing world. When we begin to think about others, we begin to love them in simple ways—first conserving and then sharing our resources. It is then that we become 'marked for mission' and join God's mission to reconcile the world.

Luke Fodor, St. John's Episcopal Church,
Cold Spring Harbor, New York

Prayers & Voices

Lord, make us instruments of your peace.
Where there is hatred, let us sow love;
    where there is injury, pardon;
    where there is discord, union;
    where there is doubt, faith;
    where there is despair, hope;
    where there is darkness, light;
    where there is sadness, joy.
Grant that we may not so much seek to be consoled as to console;
    to be understood as to understand;
    to be loved as to love.
For it is in giving that we receive;
    it is in pardoning that we are pardoned;
    and it is in dying that we are born to eternal life. Amen.

A Prayer attributed to St. Francis, BCP, p. 833

Mission is about receiving love and then responding by going out and sharing. "It is a matter of calling the near and far off together in the fold. It is about healing and reconciling. It is about making that love incarnate in the lives of people around us and in the lives of people on the other end of the earth."

The Most Reverend Katharine Jefferts Schori (1954–),
26th Presiding Bishop of The Episcopal Church

"No more wars,
No more bloodshed,
Peace unto you. Shalom, salaam, forever."

O God, you made us in your own image and redeemed us
through Jesus your Son: Look with compassion on the whole
human family; take away the arrogance and hatred which infect
our hearts; break down the walls that separate us; unite us in
bonds of love; and work through our struggle and confusion to
accomplish your purposes on earth; that, in your good time, all
nations and races may serve you in harmony around your heavenly throne; through Jesus Christ our Lord. Amen.

For the Human Family, BCP, p. 815

"Mission is really making us all aware of the incredible love that
God has for all of us. It says things like: you don't have to earn
God's love. God loves you, period. Everything flows from there."

Dios eterno, cuya voluntad es que todo vengan a tip or medio
de tu Hijo Jesucristo: Inspira el testimonio que de él damos, para
que todos conozcan el poder de su perdón y la esperanza de su
resurrección; quien vive y reina contigo y el Espíritu Santo, un
solo Dios, ahora y por siempre. Amén.

Por la mission de la Iglesia, Oraciones, BCP, p. 706

What good is it, my brothers and sisters, if you say you have faith but do not have works? Can faith save you? If a brother or sister is naked and lacks daily food, and one of you says to them, "Go in peace; keep warm and eat your fill," and yet you do not supply their bodily needs, what is the good of that? So faith by itself, it if has no works, is dead.

James 2:14–17

Think globally, act locally.

Popular bumper sticker slogan

"Never doubt that a small group of thoughtful committed citizens can change the world: Indeed, it's the only thing that ever has!"

Margaret Mead (1901–1978), anthropologist

"The Five Marks of Mission are guiding watchwords focusing on proclamation, catechesis, service, transformation, and the protection of God's creation. Worship and prayer, repentance and forgiveness, evangelism, service, and justice and peace are the five ways by which we can be about God's mission in the world. Every follower of Jesus, through baptism and in the power of the Holy Spirit, is equipped, individually and corporately as the Body of Christ, to pursue equally these five Baptismal Marks of Mission. Our baptism equips us equally to be about lives of worship and prayer, repentance and forgiveness, evangelism, service, and justice and peace as we go about God's mission of restoration and reconciliation in the world."

The Right Reverend Ian T. Douglas (1958–),
15th Diocesan Bishop of the Episcopal Diocese of Connecticut

O God, who created all peoples in your image, we thank you
for the wonderful diversity of races and cultures in this world.
Enrich our lives by ever-widening circles of fellowship, and show
us your presence in those who differ most from us, until our
knowledge of your love is made perfect in our love for all your
children; through Jesus Christ our Lord. Amen.

For the Diversity of Races and Cultures, BCP, p. 840

"Change will not come if we wait for some other person, or if we
wait for some other time. We are the ones we've been waiting
for. We are the change that we seek."

Barack Obama (1961–), 44th President of the United States

Do all the good you can,
By all the means you can,
In all the ways you can,
In all the places you can,
At all the times you can,
To all the people you can,
As long as you can.

John Wesley (1703–1791), Anglican priest and theologian

Be a gardener.
dig a ditch
toil and sweat,
and turn the earth upside down
and seek the deepness
and water the plants in time.
Continue this labor
and make sweet floods to run

and noble and abundant fruits
to spring.
Take this food and drink
and carry it to God
as your true worship.

Julian of Norwich (1342–1416), English anchoress and mystic

Creator, we give you thanks for all you are and all you bring
to us for our visit within your creation. In Jesus, you place the
Gospel in the Center of this Sacred Circle through which all of
creation is related. You show us the way to live a generous and
compassionate life. Give us your strength to live together with
respect and commitment as we grow in your spirit, for you are
God, now and forever. Amen.

Gathering Prayer, A Disciple's Prayer Book

The Beatitudes

When Jesus saw the crowds, he went up the mountain; and after
he sat down, his disciples came to him. Then he began to speak,
and taught them, saying:

"Blessed are the poor in spirit, for theirs is the kingdom
of heaven.
"Blessed are those who mourn, for they will be comforted.
"Blessed are the meek, for they will inherit the earth.
"Blessed are those who hunger and thirst for righteousness,
for they will be filled.
"Blessed are the merciful, for they will receive mercy.
"Blessed are the pure in heart, for they will see God.
"Blessed are the peacemakers, for they will be called children
of God.

"Blessed are those who are persecuted for righteousness' sake,
   for theirs is the kingdom of heaven.
"Blessed are you when people revile you and persecute you and
   utter all kinds of evil against you falsely on my account.
   Rejoice and be glad, for your reward is great in heaven, for
   in the same way they persecuted the prophets who were
   before you."

Matthew 5:1–11

Prends pitié, Père du ciel, des habitants de notre pays qui vivent
au milieu de l'injustice, de la terreur, de la maladie, de la mort.
Prends pitié de nous aussi : donne-nous ta grâce, pour ue nous
cessions de nous montrer cruels envers notre prochain. Soutiens
de ta force ceux qui passent leur vie à assurer l'égalité de tous
devant la loi et dans la vie sociale. A tous accorde d'avoir une
juste part des richesses de ce pays. Par Jésus le Christ, notre
Seigneur. Amen.

Pour less opprimés, For the Oppressed, Prières, p. 675, BCP, p. 826

O merciful Creator, your hand is open wide to satisfy the needs
of every living creature: Make us always thankful for your loving
providence; and grant that we, remembering the account that
we must one day give, may be faithful stewards of your good
gifts; through Jesus Christ our Lord, who with you and the Holy
Spirit lives and reigns, one God, for ever and ever. Amen.

Collect for Stewardship of Creation, BCP, p. 259

"If you think you are too small to make a difference, try sleeping with a mosquito."

His Holiness the 14th Dalai Lama of Tibet (1935–), spiritual leader

Almighty God, you sent your Son Jesus Christ to reconcile the world to yourself: We praise and bless you for those whom you have sent in the power of the Spirit to preach the Gospel to all nations. We thank you that in all parts of the earth a community of love has been gathered together by their prayers and labors, and that in every place your servants call upon your Name; for the kingdom and the power and the glory are yours for ever. Amen.

For the Mission of the Church, BCP, p. 838

Let us go forth,
In the goodness of our merciful Father,
In the gentleness of our brother Jesus,
In the radiance of his Holy Spirit,
In the faith of the apostles,
In the joyful praise of the angels,
In the holiness of the saints,
In the courage of the martyrs. Amen.

Celtic blessing

LIVING OUT MY FAITH

Almighty and everlasting God, by whose Spirit the whole body of your faithful people is governed and sanctified: Receive our supplications and prayers, which we offer before you for all members of your holy Church, that in their vocation and ministry they may truly and devoutly serve you; through our Lord and Savior Jesus Christ, who lives and reigns with you, in the unity of the Holy Spirit, one God, now and forever. Amen.

Book of Common Prayer, p. 256

The Charter for Lifelong Christian Formation

Through The Episcopal Church, God *Invites* all people:

- To enter into a prayerful life of worship, continuous learning, intentional outreach, advocacy, and service.

- To hear the Word of God through scripture, to honor church teachings, and continually to embrace the joy of Baptism and Eucharist, spreading the Good News of the risen Christ and ministering to all.

- To respond to the needs of our constantly changing communities, as Jesus calls us, in ways that reflect our diversity and cultures as we seek, wonder, and discover together.

- To hear what the Spirit is saying to God's people, placing ourselves in the stories of our faith, thereby empowering us to proclaim the Gospel message.

> *You did not choose me but I chose you.*
> *And I appointed you to go and bear fruit.*
> John 15:16

Through The Episcopal Church, God *Inspires* all people:

- To experience Anglican liturgy, which draws us closer to God, helps us discern God's will, and encourages us to share our faith journeys.

- To study scripture, mindful of the context of our societies and cultures, calling us to seek truth anew while remaining fully present in the community of faith.

- To develop new learning experiences, equipping disciples for life in a world of secular challenges and carefully listening for the words of modern sages who embody the teachings of Christ.

- To prepare for a sustainable future by calling the community to become guardians of God's creation.

I am giving you these commands so that you may love one another.
John 15:17

Through The Episcopal Church, God *Transforms* all people:

- By doing the work Jesus Christ calls us to do, living into the reality that we are all created in the image of God, and carrying out God's work of reconciliation, love, forgiveness, healing, justice, and peace.

- By striving to be a loving and witnessing community, which faithfully confronts the tensions in the church and the world as we struggle to live God's will.

- By seeking out diverse and expansive ways to empower prophetic action, evangelism, advocacy, and collaboration in our contemporary global context.

- By holding all accountable to lift every voice in order to reconcile oppressed and oppressor to the love of God in Jesus Christ our Lord.

Christian Faith Formation in The Episcopal Church
is a lifelong journey with Christ, in Christ, and to Christ.

Invited, inspired, transformed

Christian formation is the lifelong process of growing in relationship with God, self, others, and all creation. In this process we are transformed into the people God wants us to be. As twenty-first-century Episcopalians, we still long for the inheritance common to all Christians in all times and places — to be united in Christ, who calls us in the power of the Holy Spirit to love the Lord our God with all our heart, mind, soul, and bodies; to love our neighbors as ourselves; and to make disciples, baptize, and teach. In our Baptismal Covenant, The Episcopal Church has gracefully articulated the way in which we answer Christ's call. Lifelong Christian Formation describes the many processes by which we live into that covenant.

Through The Charter, we are invited to a life of prayer, service, education, and worship; inspired to experience our faith journey through the lens of worship, scripture, reason, and tradition; and are transformed to live into our baptismal promises, serving, witnessing, empowering, and holding all accountable.

- **To inform,** grow in knowledge of the Christian faith so that who we are and how we live is shaped and influenced by what we know.
- **To form**, we nurture our identity and lifestyle as a disciple of Christ.
- **To transform**, we promote the personal and social transformation of the world according to the kingdom of God that Jesus preached.

The Charter encourages us to actively participate in church life and to practice the Christian way of life at home and in our daily lives. Everything we do informs how we live out God's mission — worship, service, prayer, and community life. Mission then involves sharing stories as well as building hospitals; social transformation as well as personal service.

An important part of being Christian in a multi-faith society is to understand one's faith enough to be able to live in the world honoring that faith while honoring and affirming others' faith. Be it intentional or unintentional, every life experience is an opportunity to live out our Baptismal Covenant. Formation is foundational to everything we believe and do. Education is a part of formation, but it is not the only part. Stewardship, outreach, hospitality, and liturgy are all part of our formation as Christians.

It encompasses learning, action, and reflection that never ends, no matter how old we are or how much education we've had.

The Charter for Lifelong Christian Formation was adopted at General Convention in 2009 as a way to lift up the importance of continuing to learn throughout our life. It offers us many ways to continue to grow in faith, love, and service within our church community and beyond.

In Action

I find that I continue to grow in my faith by helping others grow theirs. I am a member of our Diocesan Youth Council, and one of our jobs is to lead retreats for the youth of the diocese at the Barbara C. Harris Camp and Conference Center, our diocesan camp. I think that every aspect of these retreats helps me grow in my faith, as I am constantly meeting new people and hearing their fresh ideas. For me, helping other youth to understand and form their own opinions on scripture, their faith, their life, and how they all intertwine is also helping me grow in my faith. I'm not sure who gets more out of these retreats — the retreatants or me.

Kayden Nasworthy, St. Andrew's Episcopal Church,
Ayer, Massachusetts

I have learned that living in today's society, it can be difficult to hold on to your faith. We see so much death and hate in the world today. It can be difficult to find God in all of the mess. For me, I have learned that staying positive, and always remembering that God is good helps me to never lose hope. Yes, the world is a dark place, but God is the light that is still glowing and continues to glow. Whenever I start to lose my faith I always refer to 1 Corinthians 2:9. It says, "That is what the scriptures mean when they say, no eye has seen, no ear has heard, and no mind has imagined what God has prepared for those who love him" (*New Living Translation*). This reminds me not to lose faith in God just yet. He has big things not only in store for me, but for everyone who loves him. It also has helped my faith grow, by giving all my love and trust to God.

Whitney Chapman, St. Mark's Episcopal Church,
Berkeley Springs, West Virginia

I see God through all the nurturing relationships that I have, especially with friends and family. I continue to grow in my faith by making new relationships and by trying to show love to all of God's children, especially those that may not see God's love from others often. I also grow in my faith in what I consider to be miracles. I have a simple definition of miracles; I do not expect people to walk on water so that I have to believe in God.

Over a year ago, my aunt told us she was pregnant with her first child at forty years old. She was pregnant because of the artificial insemination process she and her husband went through; they had been trying for a child for a few years. Now, I find artificial insemination a miracle. She was a high-risk pregnancy not only because of her age, but she had had open-heart surgery as a teenager. When my little cousin was born, I cried because I was so happy he was alive and healthy and now he laughs hysterically at things that fall. I know he was conceived as a miracle and his laugh still makes my faith grow.

Ariana Gonzalez-Bonillas, St. Matthew's Episcopal Church,
Chandler, Arizona

During my senior year in high school, I was in a terrible skiing accident in which I collided with a tree and broke two bones in my leg. The accident left me bedridden for several weeks, as my leg healed from surgery. To add insult to injury, my high school love broke up with me the week after the accident. I was literally in pieces: a fractured body, a shattered psyche, and a broken heart.

In the weeks that followed, I had plenty of time to be alone with my thoughts, and to begin the long process of healing.

One of the unexpected sources of healing was a casual weeknight Bible study. A few friends who had been meeting to study scripture together moved the Bible study to my house after the accident to keep me company. Every Wednesday night, a group of friends would climb in around me on the pullout sofa in my living room (the island I called home for several weeks until I could manage the stairs), and we'd select a scripture passage at random and talk about it together. Their companionship, and this ritual, grounded me. Instead of feeling lonely or depressed, I began to rejoice in the positives brought about by this experience.

Long after my bones healed, I continued to feel the physical effects from crashing into a tree with my entire body: constant neck and shoulder pain that contributed to daily headaches; a dull ache in the titanium rod in my leg every time it rained; difficulty walking long distances. Finally, I became sick of the internal monologue that said I was forever damaged. That's when I decided to take up running, which opened up a new world to me and connected me more deeply with God through moving prayer. The day that my "broken" body crossed the finish line of a half marathon, I wept from the overwhelming feeling of being freed from a great burden.

In the Church, we talk a lot about the gift of healing, but what about the gift of allowing oneself to be healed? This is something that requires trusting others, loving one's self, and listening to God. I've experienced a great deal of healing in the twelve years since my accident: physically, psychologically, and spiritually. Most importantly, though, I have come to understand that I am a beloved child of God. We all are. We may be broken, but God wants to restore us. We may be shattered, but God wants to make us whole.

Just remember to open ourselves up to healing. Let us look at our wounds, our imperfections, our heartaches, and see places where we can let light in. Where we can let love in. Where we can let God in.

Callie Swanlund, Church of St. Martin's-in-the-Fields,
Philadelphia, Pennsylvania

To continue to grow my faith, I teach a first through third grade Sunday School class at Christ Church in Dover, Delaware. Also, for the past two summers, I have worked at Camp Arrowhead. Currently I am in the process of directing the Christmas pageant at St. Thomas Parish in Newark, Delaware.

Mariah Payne, Newark, Delaware

In the midst of college life, it is hard to keep the faith. So many other things are vying for your attention. Academics, of course, take a huge amount of time. Socializing takes another huge chunk. You have to spend time taking care of all of the things mom used to do for you too, as well as making time to eat, sleep, and relax as well. It is easy to see why church and God take the back seat for a while. College is a time of questioning and change — where you form your opinions, and begin habits that follow you through adulthood; so if attending church is last on the list, where do you think it will stay?

The key is to show up. There are campus ministries of all sorts in college, as well as local churches on Sunday mornings. Go explore one. I have found welcoming communities in a local parish and among the various campus ministries, and all I did was show up. Even if it is not what you are used too, or not a place you feel at home, just show up. It builds the habit of going to church, of regular attendance, and any worship space gives you the time and place to think, to pray, and to grow. All you have to do is come. There will always be an open door.

Ben Cowgill, St. Timothy's, Winston-Salem, North Carolina

I help with a feeding ministry at my church every third Thursday of the month. I also encourage every youth within my church to get involved in youth events and pray that they open their hearts and minds to God.

Tonie Renaud, Church of the Resurrection, Miami, Florida

To help further my faith in God I try my hardest to help others in any way that I can. Little did I know that at the beginning of my junior year I would be put to the test. God put before me a situation where I could either help a person and change their life forever or leave them on their own.

My friend is a year older than me. We go to school together and have been friends since my freshman year. One day he came to me and told me that he had been living in his car for a couple of weeks. His mom was again doing drugs, and his father's (who he didn't meet until he was ten years old) house was not clean enough to live in. I knew I had to do something. I wasn't going to let him continue to live like that. I told my parents, and now he lives with us. Later I found out that he had been planning to quit school. At that moment I knew I had made the correct decision.

Margaret Milburn, Trinity Episcopal Church, Covington, Kentucky

I attend church services every Sunday, I go to church camp every summer for two to three weeks, and I attend multiple youth events throughout my diocese. I am a member of the youth council and I participate in being an acolyte, usher, greeter, and reader. All this helps me grow in my faith.

Shelby Carlton, St. Mark's Episcopal Church, Louisville, Kentucky

Faith, like so many things in life, is always changing. There are times in life that our faith is our sole pillar of strength because the world has become a dark place. Other times, our faith may be wavering because as humans we are always questioning. It is so important to seek out answers and nourishment for our body, mind, and spirit.

Recently, I acknowledged that I do not have love for scripture. I often find that people abuse the text to make it fit their own agendas, and so I have had some disdain toward throwing myself into it. After I met a priest who I could really get direction from I have found what works for me. She introduced me to a technique of reading that allows me to put myself into the scene that the Gospels portray; the Latin term is *Lectio Divina*. It may not be for everyone, but it helps me be able to see.

Kate Riley, Emmanuel Episcopal Church, Cumberland, Maryland

Of course, scripture study and prayer are both important in my faith life, but a new routine for my faith growth is reading. Not theological studies or commentaries on the Bible, but reading every day pieces of writing, whether it's "Harry Potter," "The Hunger Games," poetry by T. S. Eliot, or short stories by Ernest Hemingway. Christianity is about relationships. The Bible gives me a wonderful insight into my relationship with God, and also with other people, but I have found literature to be one of the best ways to understand your relationships with others. It gives you a new perspective into a person's life, or how they might react to situations. So, constantly reading helps me to continue to grow in my faith.

Thomas Alexander, St. Margaret's Episcopal Church,
Little Rock, Arkansas

Being in college, it is sometimes difficult to get up early on Sundays and go to church. However, I feel empty when I don't attend and share my love for Christ with the members of my community. I am currently at a school that is almost 500 miles away from my home church and am attending a parish that is just as welcoming. No matter where you are you can find a church community that will love you and take care of you, even if that means having members of the choir drive you to and from the airport for breaks, to and from choir rehearsals, and even offer their homes when you feel homesick or just want a home-cooked meal. These people have taught me that there is kindness in unfamiliar places; one just has to know where to look. And when coffee is involved and fun worship filled with love, how could you pass it up?

Elizabeth L. Engle, St. Matthias Episcopal Church,
East Aurora, New York

I have been organizing youth mission trips for years: coordinating Vacation Bible School (VBS) for inner-city children in Washington DC, painting houses on the Wind River Reservation, digging trenches for new homes in Costa Rica, and cleaning marsh areas of Mississippi after Hurricane Katrina.

During all of these trips I have witnessed incredible strength and maturity in the lives of the young people traveling with me.

But it was not until the summer of 2007 in Bay Saint Lewis with 150 youth from Province IV did I begin to truly understand the greatest gift any of us can give.

As photographer for the week, I came to a group of youth pulling weeds at Malcolm's home, his roof covered with a blue tarp and much of the siding torn away. The youth asked Malcolm to tell the story about how his neighbors had planned to end their lives after seeing the devastation from Katrina. With tears rolling down his face, Malcolm said to us, "The idea of how valuable you are to us I think is quite simple: you give us hope."

This hope Malcolm experienced with the youth from Province IV came out of genuine relationships built through sharing work, laughter, tears, stories, and most importantly love with one another. Yes, the work done during these mission experiences is important and much appreciated. However, it's the relationships developed during these experiences that last a lifetime.

My hope is that through mission we build these ongoing relationships across the vastness and diversity of our church and that through these relationships we transform our communities, our world, and ourselves.

Beth Crow, Youth Missioner for the
Episcopal Diocese of North Carolina

Over this past summer, I was working at the Barbara C. Harris Camp in New Hampshire. Events took place, and a couple dumb decisions were made. Nothing was done like super wrong against the Ten Commandments, but I did break a few camp rules. Long story short, I was fired. This felt terrible. I felt terrible. I mean, this job was something I had always wanted to do.

I loved camp and had been going there for nine years. I always looked up to my counselors, and wanted to be like them. Now it was my turn to serve in that role, and be the leader and role model for others. I was so excited, and I couldn't wait for the best part of my summer to begin.

Seriously though, who doesn't like getting paid to play games all day? And yeah the pay wasn't great, but it was never about the pay. It was always about the people, the experiences you can't get anywhere else, and those memories that will last a lifetime. Instead, this job made me feel like a huge disappointment to so many people, especially my parents, friends, and the camp community. I became so focused on myself because of all of this. I bet if anybody had asked me to help them through their own problems, I probably would have laughed in their face or broken down, hysterically crying.

But even though I was upset, that didn't stop me from seeing my heroes come to save me. I had been fired on a Sunday morning, and asked to leave before 2:00 p.m. But before I left, some friends stopped me. At first, it was only a couple other counselors who just asked what was wrong, not knowing about the weight I carried and why.

I just barely managed to tell them that I had to leave. It was so hard to mutter because I never thought I'd have to say those words. However, that meant nothing, because as soon as the words left my lips, and a moment was given for them to absorb what they just heard, all of my friends just began saying some of the greatest things to me like, "You're such a great person." "You shouldn't let this bring you down." "Have a great senior year if I don't see you anytime soon." "We're all hoping the best for you, you're an incredible person." "I love you." "If you need someone to talk to, I am here for you if and when you need me."

Almost everyone I saw came over and gave me a big hug; those who weren't sure why, and even those who were aware of what was going on at the time. And when we embraced, they gave me a few more words of encouragement and comfort.

In one particular case, I got a Facebook message from someone, and in a lengthy message. It said something that really got me through some of the toughest parts. She said, "Bad things happen, we grow, we learn, we move on. So many of us are praying for you and are so thankful you were here this summer. You are a part of this BCH family, and no matter what I know, many of us still believe you to be a part of this community . . . You are awesome, sending good thoughts your way."

It was little things like this that really pulled me through such a tough lesson and helped me to learn how to be a hero again. It taught me that our heroes don't make bad things go away, they just struggle through them with us. They don't live without fear, in it, or out of it, and they never try and put themselves above, below, in front, or behind us through their actions. They just go through life alongside us, with us, protecting us when necessary.

The other lesson this taught me is how to be a hero like all those around me who helped me through this experience, and who are still helping me through it, too. They are heroes to me. Their lives are lessons on how I can help others. When I see someone struggling, I think of my struggle.

Being on the other end now, I know that I need to help them and be the hero they need. Because that's what a hero is. Heroes are people who are willing to listen to us, to empathize with us, and to help pull us through tough times. It's a gift, and this "super power" is inside of each of us, and it is just waiting for us to share it with someone else. And of course we cannot always be perfect. Some days, we mess up. Sometimes, we fall down. But why do we fall? So we can learn to pick ourselves back up. Just because you can't be a hero every single day, it doesn't mean you can never be a hero.

Every saint has a past, and every sinner has a future. I'm a living example of that, and I am no different from any of you. That is my challenge to you. Try to be a saint. Try to live heroically. Look back at those times when you messed up. Learn from them. But most importantly, I challenge you to look for your heroes, and see how you can be like them, and how you can be someone else's hero.

Seaver Boyce, Grace Episcopal Church, New Bedford, Massachusetts

I give myself as a servant daily in my work at the parish, diocesan, and provincial level. However, I believe the best way for me to grow in my own faith is to let others, friends and siblings in Christ, into my own community so we all can thrive and grow from each others' experiences.

Austin Hays, St. Simon and St. Jude Episcopal Church,
Irmo, South Carolina

Values to Live By
You are God's loving creation.
Love God; love your neighbor as yourself.
Make Christ the center of your life.
You are never alone; God is with you always.
Seek out a family member, a friend, your priest, a teacher, and your parish family.
Believe in God; believe in yourself.
Stay in school; make your life count for something.

Do good work; strive for excellence.

Know where you come from; make wise choices for your future.

Lose the words "I can't."

Respect yourself; respect others.

Choose a role model; be a role model.

Diffuse a bad situation; say, "I'm sorry."

Help someone else on the way.

Be on time always.

Dress for success.

You have power; claim it!

Let no one but you define you.

Seize the moment; a lost opportunity does not come back.

Be a leader.

Value your life and that of others.

Assert yourself.

Angela S. Ifill, Missioner, Office of Black Ministries

A Covenant of Faith

We joyfully covenant ourselves to the continuing mission of Christ as it finds both meaning and expression in the Indigenous peoples and The Episcopal Church, with these statements of our faith:

I. As we strive for justice in reconciling our history of colonialism and the suffering it has engendered for generations between us: We will continue to be as constant in our search for the truth as we are responsive to its discoveries.

II. As we work together to find new solutions to the social and political challenges before us: We will continue to be as dedicated to the principles of self-determination as we are committed to justice for all humanity.

III. As we expand the theological and spiritual dialogue between our several traditions and communities: We will continue to be as respectful of the integrity of Indigenous traditions as we are loving in sharing Christ.

IV. As we stand together to honor, protect, and nurture our home, the Earth: We will continue to be as active in Stewardship of God's creation as we are diligent in our advocacy for its care.

Excerpt from the Office of Indigenous Ministries
of The Episcopal Church

Let me start out by confessing something to you: I'm obsessed with *Downton Abbey*. I love the clothes, the music, and the Dowager Countess' witty one-liners. Unfortunately, the period drama both romanticizes and removes the viewer from the harsh realities of life as a servant. I work with foreign domestic workers in Hong Kong. Thousands of women leave their homes and families every day to go overseas to be modern-day servants for employers who are much less gracious and appreciative than Lord Grantham and his family. Extreme poverty in their home countries motivates courageous women to endure verbal and physical abuse, harsh working conditions, a complete lack of privacy, and almost total separation from their loved ones just to provide basic necessities for their families back home.

On Maundy Thursday, scripture and tradition dictate that we pause and examine how we serve one another. John 13 describes Jesus washing his disciples' feet. In a time when walking in sandals was the main form of transportation, it's hard to imagine a much more humbling act of service than feet washing. And yet, as I listen to the stories of the women who come to the walk-in center where I work requesting advice and counsel, crying as they tell their stories, and seeking shelter from harmful situations, the more and more I'm convinced that service is sacrifice. Being a servant is more than just getting dirty, or taking on a job that no one else wants to do; it's about loving someone else so much that you're willing to sacrifice—really sacrifice time, talent, and treasure—for that other person's well-being and betterment. Jesus calls us to love one another. He goes so far as to say that we will be known as his followers if we love each other.

On Maundy Thursday we observe service. On Good Friday we observe sacrifice. Love binds those two concepts together. Without love, service and sacrifice are meaningless. As we reflect on Jesus' call to service and to love, may we remember those who sacrifice more than we can imagine with the simple desire of providing for their families.

Grace Flint served on a one-year assignment with the Young Adult Service Corps in Hong Kong from 2012–2013 with Mission for Migrant Workers.

Prayers & Voices

Dear God, Spirit, Divine Mother, you who have brought us together to know your glory and hear your word, bless us in our mission to tell, teach, tend, transform, and treasure your creation. May we be engulfed in your love and blessing. Amen.

by Ariana Gonzalez-Bonillas

Heavenly Father, giver of every good gift, grant us the tools to accomplish your mission so we may tell the Good News as you have told us of your unconditional love. Help us to teach and nurture all believers as your Son has taught us and to tend to the human condition as you, the Good Shepherd, have tended to our spirits. Guide us as we seek to transform and reconcile our world as your Son has done by His sacrifice and to treasure your creation, our earthly blessings, and our salvation by your son, Jesus Christ, in whose name we pray. Amen.

by Joseph Prickett

Ever loving God, who empowered the apostles with your spirit, we ask you to empower us as we seek to tell the Gospel, to teach those around us, to tend all you have created, to transform unjust structures, and to treasure all the work you have called us to do. Through Jesus Christ, who lives with you and the Holy Spirit for ever and ever. Amen

by Lillian Hardaway and Thomas Alexander

"Everybody can be great . . . because anybody can serve. You don't have to have a college degree to serve. You don't have to make your subject and verb agree to serve. You only need a heart full of grace. A soul generated by love."

The Reverend Dr. Martin Luther King Jr. (1929–1968),
civil rights leader

O God, from whom all good proceeds: Grant that by our inspiration we may think those things that are right, and by your merciful guiding may do them; through Jesus Christ our Lord, who lives and reigns with you and the Holy Spirit, one God, for ever and ever. Amen.

Collect for Proper 5, BCP, p. 229

Ever loving God, you have brought us together and empowered us to serve as your disciples. We ask you to guide and bless us as we strive to tell the Good News of your love; teach and nurture all believers; tend to the human condition; transform and reconcile the world as Christ has shown us; and treasure your creation and our salvation through Jesus Christ. May we be engulfed in your love and blessings as we live out the mission and work you have given us, through Jesus Christ, who lives with you and the Holy Spirit forever and ever. Amen.

by the Liturgy and Music Team of EYE 2014

Almighty and eternal God, so draw our hearts to you, so guide our minds, so fill our imaginations, so control our wills, that we may be wholly yours, utterly dedicated to you; and then use us, we pray, as you will, and always to your glory and the welfare of your people; through our Lord and Savior Jesus Christ. Amen.

A Prayer of Self-Dedication, BCP, p. 832

Christ has no body but yours, no hands but yours, no feet
but yours.
Yours are the eyes through which Christ's compassion looks
out on the world.
Yours are the feet with which he is to go about doing good.
And yours are the hands with which he is to bless us now.

St. Teresa of Ávila, Spanish mystic and Carmelite nun (1515–1582)

Almighty and everliving God,
we thank you for feeding us with the spiritual food
of the most precious Body and Blood
of your Son our Savior Jesus Christ;
and for assuring us in these holy mysteries
that we are living members of the Body of your Son,
and heirs of your eternal kingdom.
And now, Father, send us out
to do the work you have given us to do,
to love and serve you
as faithful witnesses of Christ our Lord.
To him, to you, and to the Holy Spirit,
be honor and glory, now and for ever. Amen.

Post-Communion Prayer, BCP, p. 366

Pentecost: The Holy Spirit Came
Holy Spirit, you came to us in every language of every culture
and every nation.
Pour out your power upon our divisions.
Make us remember that every tongue is a reflection of your
creation.
You converted our babble of sounds into speech.

You made our difference become our hope. But we have run
   away from each other,
And have created enclaves of race, color, and creed.
Bring us back to a place where we can hear you, see you,
And feel your presence in every ocean, hill, mountain, and
   valley. And we pray this in your name. Amen.

from "Race and Prayer: Collected Voices, Many Dreams," p. 115

"Leadership and learning are indispensable to each other."

John F. Kennedy (1917–1963), 35th President of the United States

Gracious and Holy Father,
give us wisdom to perceive you,
diligence to seek you,
patience to wait for you,
eyes to behold you,
a heart to meditate on you
and a life to proclaim you,
through the power of the Spirit
of Jesus Christ our Lord. Amen.

St. Benedict of Nursia (c. 480–543), founder of western monasticism

"Be the change that you wish to see in the world."

*Mohandas Karamchand Gandhi (1869–1948), Hindu leader
of India who practiced non-violent civil disobedience*

"For attractive lips, speak words of kindness.
For lovely eyes, seek out the good in people.
For a slim figure, share your food with the hungry.
For beautiful hair, let a child run their fingers through it once
    a day.
For poise, walk with the knowledge that you never walk alone.
People, more than things, have to be restored, renewed,
      revived, reclaimed, and redeemed. Remember, if you
      ever need a helping hand, you will find one at the end
      of each of your arms.
As you grow older, you will discover that you have two hands,
    one for helping yourself and the other for helping others."

Sam Levenson, American writer and journalist (1911–1980)

"Anyone who stops learning is old, whether at twenty or eighty.
Anyone who keeps learning stays young."

Henry Ford (1863–1947), American industrialist

Dios todopoderoso y eterno, de tal modo atrae nuestro corazón
hacia ti, dirige nuestra mente, inspira nuestra imaginación y
gobierna nuestra voluntad, que seamos totalmente tuyos, dedi-
cados por complete a ti. Te rogamos nos uses según tu voluntad,
y siepre para tu Gloria y el bienestar de tu pueblo; por Jesucristo
nuestro Señor y Salvador. Amen.

Acto de dedicación personal, Oraciones, BCP, p. 724

"Education is the kindling of a flame, not the filling of a vessel."

Socrates (c. 469–399 BCE), Ancient Greek philosopher

Lord Jesus,
you know each of us by name
and have called us to follow you;
teach us how to respond anew
in every opportunity this day will bring.
We ask you this, you who love us
with the Father and the Spirit,
for ever and ever.

Collect for Tuesday from "A Celtic Primer," p. 59

"This is my commandment, that you love one another as I have loved you. No one has greater love than this, to lay down one's life for one's friends. You are my friends if you do what I command you. I do not call you servants any longer, because the servant does not know what the master is doing; but I have called you friends, because I have made known to you everything that I have heard from my Father. You did not choose me but I chose you. And I appointed you to go and bear fruit, fruit that will last, so that the Father will give you whatever you ask him in my name. I am giving you these commands so that you may love one another."

John 15:12–17

RESOURCES

Teach me good judgment and knowledge, for I believe in your commandments.

Psalm 119:66

The Bible

Throughout the rich history of the Church, the Bible has stood as the foundation for belief and practice. The worship and work of the Church, in all its diversity, have been based on the Word of God inspired by the Holy Spirit working through human hands. Derived from the Greek *biblia* ("books"), the Bible is a library of sixty-six books that share the history and story of God's relationship to all of creation and our relationship with God.

We believe God is still writing. We are alert to ways the Living God continues to inform us and communicate with us. There are many translations of the Bible from scholars and committees who have sought to bring the original Hebrew, Aramaic, Syriac, and Latin writings to our language as correctly as possible. In The Episcopal Church, we typically use the New Revised Standard Version (NRSV) in worship and are beginning to embrace the Common English Bible (CEB) version as most accurate to the original biblical writings. Our quest for authorship of the Bible is ongoing, as is our search for the ways God continues to speak and actively move in our lives. We may not tend to take the Bible literally, but we do take it seriously.

Major themes can be found throughout the books of the Bible, including creation, covenant, and salvation. These themes are also found in our Baptismal Covenant and the Five Marks of Mission. Through scripture, God's people are called again and again to renew a right relationship with God. Beginning with the story of creation in the book of Genesis, we hear stories of how God's people forgot their purpose and were separated from

God, only to be called back by individuals who were considered "righteous" such as Noah, and Abraham. The Hebrew Scriptures (Old Testament) share the stories of these people who continually seek freedom; freedom to be the people God intended them to be. Moses led them across the Red Sea waters to freedom, much like we are brought to new life through the waters of baptism.

The New Testament (Christian Scriptures) tells how God became incarnate, with us, in Jesus Christ so that we may be united with God for all time. As God's Chosen, Jesus' ministry of healing and teaching becomes the means of God's blessing for others. Jesus calls others to discipleship, and commissions them with a task that echoes the call of those ancestors we have heard speaking to us throughout scripture. All of us are called to become a source of blessing to others.

Reading Scripture

The subject of the Bible can bring anxiety for Christians. Some followers know the Bible well; I've met people who can recite all 66 books in the Bible. Other followers know relatively little about the Bible; sometimes there's guilt associated with this. Myself, although I've done some studying of the Bible, I continue to learn more and more about scripture.

I remember the first Bible verse I ever memorized. I remember because it was the first Bible verse my friend in college memorized. I was pained over some problem I was having. (I can't remember what the problem was, so it shows its relative importance compared to the Bible verse.) My friend was patiently listening. I finally stopped whining, and she told me the Bible verse.

Don't be anxious about anything; rather, bring up all of your requests to God in your prayers and petitions, along with giving thanks. Then the peace of God that exceeds all understanding will keep your hearts and minds safe in Christ Jesus. (Philippians 4:6–7, CEB)

First, I couldn't believe she had memorized such a long verse. She said it's the only one she knew; she found it important. Also, I was surprised how it fit the place I was in, and what I was looking for. What does the verse say? The verse tells a worrier not to worry. It gives a roadmap on how to deal with hard things in life. And it has a promise: peace. A special kind of peace, only from God. This is my favorite part of the verse; God's peace is beyond human understanding. God has a clock and a planner well beyond our own. We don't know why things happen the way they do. We don't know. Only God knows. And we are not God.

But God promises peace in the midst of this not knowing. Believing the peace of God can come to me comforted me then.

Rob Johnson, Minnesota

A dispute also arose among them as to which one of them was to be regarded as the greatest. But he said to them, "The kings of the Gentiles lord it over them; and those in authority over them are called benefactors. But not so with you; rather the greatest among you must become like the youngest, and the leader like one who serves. For who is greater, the one who is at the table or the one who serves? Is it not the one at the table? But I am among you as one who serves." (Luke 22:24–27)

Rosanna Vizcaino, La transfiguracion Bani,
Provincia Peravia, Republica Dominicana

My favorite book to refer to for everything is my *Student's Life Application Bible*. When I'm completely lost with a scripture or need some guidance, I always refer to my Bible. What I appreciate with my Bible is that it is broken down in a way that I'm able to understand what is being said. I think sometimes it can be very difficult to understand what God wants us to hear when the language is complex. I believe that if I were having a conversation with God he would have a normal conversation with me just like anyone else. That's why I appreciate my *Student's Life Application Bible*.

Whitney Chapman, St. Mark's Episcopal Church,
Berkeley Springs, West Virginia

but those who wait for the LORD shall renew their strength,
they shall mount up with wings like eagles,
they shall run and not be weary,
they shall walk and not faint. (Isaiah 40:31)

This is my favorite Bible verse, because it reminds me of the song "On Eagle's Wings." November 26, 2012, I lost my sixteen-year-old friend Jantz to a dirt biking accident. This was the song that they played as they pushed his casket down the aisle at the funeral. It reminds me that he is in a better place, where he can ride on endless dirt bike trails. We all miss him so much, but I truly believe that the Lord lifted him up on eagle's wings.

Cydney Jackson, St. Bartholomew's Episcopal Church,
Poway, California

Prayer

Prayer is our conversation with God. It can be formal and informal, spoken or sung, loud or silent. Prayer can be individual or communal. In The Episcopal Church, we can trace our liturgical (worship) prayers to the first Book of Common Prayer written by Archbishop Thomas Cranmer in 1549. Anglicans use this book, revised many times over the years, throughout the world, with their own editions created to fit the context and needs of each locality.

The Episcopal Church uses a version of the Book of Common Prayer published in 1979. We call it "common prayer" because we can all say it together. It includes worship services, such as Morning Prayer, Holy Baptism, Holy Eucharist, and Compline. It also contains a number of prayers for all needs and occasions. When we come together for worship with others, we are following Jesus' example, "For when two or three are gathered in my name, I am there among them" (Matthew 18:20). No matter where you are, when you pray these common prayers, you are not alone. You are praying with many others around the world as one body with Christ.

We can also pray in our own words, offering thanks or praise, or asking forgiveness or help for others or ourselves. Think of the acronym ACTS when you pray: adoration, thanksgiving, confession, and supplication. Give praise to God, give thanks to God, say you're sorry to God (and others), and offer prayers on behalf of those in need: the sick, the hurting, the homeless, and all who we hold in our hearts.

Youth Mission Commissioning Service

Celebrant (to the congregation): Almighty God, you raise up laborers for your harvest, sending them out as sowers of your good news, workers of healing, and caretakers of your people: Bless these young missioners as they work to bring about your kingdom in (insert name of destination).

Celebrant (to the teens and leaders): (Insert names of youth and adult participants), as you undertake this service, will you spread the good news of Christ by your words and actions, keeping in mind that you are ambassadors of (insert your church's name), the Diocese of (insert your diocese's name), and more importantly, Jesus Christ?

Missioners: We will, with God's help.

Celebrant (to the congregation): Let us pray for our youth and their mission work: Loving God, equip these young people for your service, enliven them with your joy, keep them safe while they work and play in your Name, and help them to remember that their help is always in you, through Jesus Christ, our redeemer and steadfast companion. Amen.

From the Episcopal Diocese of North Carolina

A Service of Thanksgiving and Commissioning

Psalm 134
Behold now, bless the Lord, all you servants of the Lord,*
you that stand by night in the house of the Lord.
Lift up your hands in the holy place and bless the Lord;*
the Lord who made heaven and earth bless you out of Zion.

Litany of Thanksgiving
Let us give thanks to God for all God's gifts so freely bestowed
upon us. For the beauty and wonder of your creation, in earth
and sky and sea,
We thank you Lord.

For all that is gracious in the lives of men, women, and children,
revealing the image of Christ,
We thank you Lord.

For our daily food and drink, our homes and families, and our
friends,
We thank you Lord.

For minds to think, and hearts to love, and hands to serve,
We thank you Lord.

For health and strength to work, and leisure to rest and play,
We thank you Lord.

For the brave and courageous, who are patient in suffering and faithful in adversity,
We thank you Lord.

For all valiant seekers after truth, liberty, and justice,
We thank you Lord.

For the communion of saints, in all times and places,
We thank you Lord.

For those who have gone forth from our congregation to witness to your glory and goodness in the lives of all people. We give thanks especially for those who went to (add names of previous mission locations), and offered themselves to the building up and care of (name projects, people, communities served). We give thanks for their offering, the friendships made, the bonds of love extended to them and for their safe return. Help us, to be like them, your faithful servants and active participants in the building up of your realm on earth. Above all, we give you thanks for the great mercies and promises given to us in Christ Jesus our Lord; to him be praise and glory, with you, O Father and the Holy Spirit, now and for ever. Amen.

The Commissioning:

Celebrant or Officiant: Brothers and Sisters in Christ Jesus, we are all baptized by the one Spirit into one Body, and given gifts for a variety of ministries for the common good. We gather to commission these persons in the Name of God and of this congregation to a special ministry to which they are called.

Sponsor: I present to you these persons to be ambassadors for Christ on behalf of this congregation. They have been preparing to go on a mission trip to (place) to form friendships and to (name mission project or community to which they are going).

Celebrant to those called: You have been called on behalf of your congregation to go out as witnesses to the Risen Christ, as His ambassadors, to uphold and seek to serve Christ in all persons and places. Through Christ and with Him, you will share in a ministry of reconciliation and encouragement, to build up the body of Christ and to care for all who come to Him. Will you faithfully and reverently carry out this ministry to the honor of God and the benefit of this community and all whom you serve?

Candidates: I will.

Celebrant: Let us pray. Gracious God, your Son before he ascended to glory declared that your people would receive power from the Holy Spirit to bear witness to him to the ends of the earth: Be present with all who go forth in his Name, protect them all the day long and bring them safely home. Let your love shine through their witness, so that all who come to them may see your glory in all that is given, through Jesus Christ our Lord. Amen.

Almighty God, look with favor upon these persons who have now reaffirmed their commitment to follow Christ and to serve in his name. Give them courage, patience, and vision; and strengthen us all in our Christian vocation of witness to the world, and of service to others; through Jesus Christ our Lord. Amen.

In the Name of God and of this congregation, I commission you, (names), as ambassadors and missionaries. Let your light so shine before others that they may see your good works and give glory to God. I commend you to this work, and pledge you our prayers, encouragement, and support. The almighty and merciful Lord, Father, Son and Holy Spirit, bless us and keep us. Amen.

From the Charles River Deanery in the Episcopal Diocese of Massachusetts

Praying

I am in love with the Daily Office presented in our Book of
Common Prayer. I prayed daily through my senior year of
high school with members of my church, and it proved to be a
formative experience of my journey so far. Not only did I take
the beginning of my day to connect with God, but also I grew
in faith alongside people who I now call close friends and mentors. I memorized parts of the text, not on purpose, but by simple
repetition, and heard new parts of the Bible through daily read-
ings. Praying the Daily Office is something I would encourage
anyone to try, because it puts you in the habit of worship and
brings your relationship to God to a whole new level.

Ben Cowgill, St. Timothy's, Winston-Salem, North Carolina

I have been called the prayer-book police, so my obvious resource would be the Book of Common Prayer. It is a living docu-
ment of many generations and cultures, all tied together by the
love of God and scripture. Just imagine how many people have
been baptized, blessed, healed, married, ordained, and buried
with the words "in the name of the Father, and of the Son, and
of the Holy Spirit." The Book of Common Prayer is a physical
reminder to the Church that we are an everlasting communion.
The prayers I say from that book make me feel a part of a larger
body that supports and loves the work I do each and every day.

Thomas Alexander, St. Margaret's Episcopal Church,
Little Rock, Arkansas

Common Prayer: A Liturgy for Ordinary Radicals by Shane Claiborne, Jonathan Wilson-Hartgrove. It resembles the Episcopal Book of Common Prayer, which I really like, but also gives examples of other forms of worship, and people who you may not have thought of as an example to look up to.

Kate Riley, Emmanuel Episcopal Church, Cumberland, Maryland

Early in my ministry with children and youth, I acquired a copy of Marian Wright Edelman's *Guide My Feet: Prayers and Meditations on Loving and Working for Children*. Edelman is the founder and president of the Children's Defense Fund. Her preface to *Guide My Feet* is one of the most helpful pieces I have ever read about putting your faith in action because you were raised in a community of faithful people. As a parent and a youth minister, I have found her prayers and meditations incredibly helpful over the years; I find myself reaching for her book, even when worrying over my adult children and godchildren. My favorite prayer of hers is on the back cover jacket for the book. I offer this prayer for you.

> God, help me to be honest
> so my children will learn honesty.
> Help me to be kind
> so my children will learn kindness.
> Help me to be faithful
> so my children will learn faith.
> Help me to love
> so my children will be loving.

Bronwyn Clark Skov, Hastings, Minnesota

The first time I visited an Episcopal Church was a little over a year ago when I went to an Evening Prayer service. I was raised in the Roman Catholic tradition, and I was very familiar with the practice of the Divine Office. At this time in my life I began asking some deep and difficult questions about my spiritual journey that seemingly pushed me further away from my Roman Catholic tradition, and, for some reason, pulled me closer to the Episcopal tradition. One day I finally decided to feed my curiosity about The Episcopal Church, and I walked into the darkened sanctuary one cold winter night to join a small community of about four for Evening Prayer. I had long set down my breviary from which I used to recite Morning and Evening Prayer. This practice had, for a long time, lost its "taste" for me, but that night renewed my appreciation of the practice. That week I went out to buy my own personal copy of the Book of Common Prayer, and the practice of praying Morning and Evening Prayer has become a routine in my daily life that is more than an empty recitation of prayers.

For me, it not only connects me to the common prayer of the wider Church, but it also allows me to set aside time in the day to recognize God's loving presence in my day-to-day life. Whenever I pray Morning or Evening Prayer out of my Book of Common Prayer, I think of it as joining my brothers and sisters throughout the Anglican Communion who also are simply giving thanks and relishing in the day that we have been given by our Creator. It is a way for me, and for us as a Church, to simply give recognition to the fact that we rely on God's grace every day, and that we are dependent upon our Creator who gives us the ultimate gift of the day we are living in right now!

The Book of Common Prayer, with its accessible richness, is what first embraced me and welcomed me into The Episcopal

Church. The Liturgy of Morning and Evening Prayer is truly "the work of the people," and it is a treasury of grace that gives my day life and space to commune with God and God's Church in a profoundly simple way.

Trenton Hale, St. Stephen's Episcopal Church, Huntsville, Texas

I have a prayer by Debbie Ford that starts with "Dear God, Spirit, Divine Mother" that keeps me centered on my own and God's holiness. It keeps me aware of my actions, brave, humble, looking for the highest truth, loving myself, and choosing faith over fear. I pray this when in desperation and in happiness, in strong emotions, but also every time I pray simply for faith.

Ariana Gonzalez-Bonillas, St. Matthew's Episcopal Church, Chandler, Arizona

May the road rise up to meet you.
May the wind always be at your back.
May the sun shine warm upon your face,
and rains fall soft upon your fields.
And until we meet again,
May God hold you in the palm of His hand.

I love this Irish Blessing. I have this prayer posted in my room and I read it daily and it refreshes me and focuses me.

I try to do the devotion everyday on d365.org. It doesn't take long and it helps me focus on what I want to be that day. It reminds me to be kind and patient. I like how it gives scripture, a short explanation, and a prayer that sends you out.

Lillian Hardaway, Grace Episcopal Church, Anderson, South Carolina

God of the dirtied hands, the wandering feet; you seek out
the lost before ever they turn to you: take us with you into the
abandoned places to find a new community outside your fortress
walls; through Jesus Christ, the Searching One. Amen.

Collect for Proper 19, Year C from
"Prayers for An Inclusive Church," p. 105

Open my lips, O Lord, and my mouth shall proclaim your praise.
Create in me a clean heart, O God, and renew a right spirit
    within me.
Cast me not away from your presence and take not your holy
    Spirit from me.
Give me the joy of your saving help again and sustain me with
    your bountiful Spirit.
Glory to the Father, and to the Son, and to the Holy Spirit: as it
    was in the beginning, is now, and will be for ever. Amen.

Psalm 51:16, 11–13 BCP, 657

O Christ, you are the dawn and day
before whom the darkest night gives way,
illuminating all our sight,
the source of faith and light of light.

To you, O blessed One, we pray,
defend us at the close of day;
may all our rest be found in you,
and peace be with us all night through.

O Christ, remember us, we cry,
who now as mortals live and die;
you, our souls' keeper and our friend,
be present with us to the end.

Creator, grant that this be done
through Jesus, your Beloved One,
who, with the Spirit and with you,
shall live and reign all ages through. Amen.

Alternative hymn for Compline, The Saint Helena Breviary

The Lord's Prayer (English Traditional)

Our Father, who art in heaven,
    hallowed be thy Name,
    thy kingdom come,
    thy will be done,
      on earth as it is in heaven.
Give us this day our daily bread.
And forgive us our trespasses,
    as we forgive those
    who trespass against us.
And lead us not into temptation,
    but deliver us from evil.
For thine is the kingdom,
    and the power, and the glory,
    for ever and ever. Amen.

The Lord's Prayer (French)

Notre Père, qui es aux cieux,
que ton Nom soit sanctifié,
que ton règne vienne,
que ta volonté soit faite sur la terre
    comme au ciel.
Donne-nous aujourd'hui notre pain de ce jour.
Pardonne-nous nos offenses,
    comme nous pardonnons aussi
      à ceux qui nous ont offensés.
Et ne nous soumets pas à la tentation,
mais deliver-nous du mal.
Car c'est à toi qu'appartiennent le règne,
la puissance et la gloire, dans les siècles des siècles. Amen.

The Lord's Prayer (Lakota)

Ate uŋyaŋpi, maȟpiya ekta naŋke cin,
Nicaje wakaŋ-lapi nuŋwe.
Nito-kicoŋze u nuŋwe.
Maȟpiya ekta nita-wa-ciŋ ecoŋpi kiŋ,
he iyecel maka akaŋl ecoŋpi nuŋwe.
Aŋpetu iyohi aǵuyapi kiŋ, aŋpetu kiŋ le uŋqu piye.
Na tona eciŋśni-yaŋ ecauŋ-kiciŋpi
wicauŋ-kici-ca-juju-pi kiŋ,
he iyecel wauŋ-ȟta-nipi kiŋ,
uŋki-ci-ca-juju piye.

Na taku wawi-yu-taŋye cin ekta uŋkayapi śin piye;
Tka taku śice etaŋhaŋ euŋ-klaku piye;
Woki-coŋze kiŋ, na wowa-śake kiŋ, na wowitaŋ kiŋ, hena
ohiŋ-niyaŋ na ohiŋ-niyaŋ nitawa heoŋ. Amen.

The Lord's Prayer (Hmong)

Peb Txiv nyob saum ntuj.
   Koj lub npe Ntshiab nto moo lug.
   Koj lub Ceeb Tsheej los txog,
   kom muaj raws li koj nyiam nyob ntiaj teb no,
      zoo li nyob saum ntuj.
Thov koj pub mov txaus peb noj hnub no.
Koj zam rau peb. Zoo li peb zam rau luag.
   Thaum dab phem tuaj ntxias peb siab,
Koj txhob tso peb tseg,
   Ua kom peb dim ntawm tus phem.
Kev ua Vaj, kev muaj hwj huam,
   kev nto koob meej yog koj tug
      mus tas ib txhiab ib txhis. Ua li.

The Lord's Prayer (Contemporary English)

Our Father in heaven,
    hallowed be your Name,
    your kingdom come,
    your will be done,
      on earth as in heaven.
Give us today our daily bread.
Forgive us our sins
    as we forgive those
      who sin against us.
Save us from the time of trial,
    and deliver us from evil.
For the kingdom, the power,
    and the glory are yours,
      now and for ever. Amen.

The Lord's Prayer (Dakota)

Ate unyanpi, maȟpiya ekta nanke cin, Nicaje wakandapi
nunwe. Nitokiconze u nunwe. Maȟpiya ekta nitawacin
econpi kin, He iyecen maka akan econpi nunwe. Anpetu
iyohi aguyapi kin, anpetu kin de unqu miye. Qa tona
ecinśniyan ecaunkiconpi wicunkicicajujupi kin, He iyecen
waunȟtanipi kin unkicicajuju miye, Qa taku wawiyutanye
cin ekta unkayapi śni miye; Tka taku śice cin etanhan
eunkdaku miye: Wokiconze kin, qa wowaśake kin, qa
wowitan kin, hena ohinni qa ohinni nitawa heon. Amen.

The Lord's Prayer (Spanish)

Padre nuestro que estás en el cielo,
    santificado sea tu Nombre,
    venga tu reino,
    hágase tu voluntad,
     en la tierra como en el cielo.
Danos hoy nuestro pan de cada día.
Perdona nuestras ofensas,
    como también nosotros perdonamos
     a los que nos ofenden.
No nos dejes caer en tentación
    y líbranos del mal.
Porque tuo es el reino,
    tuyo es el poder,
    y tuya es la Gloria,
    ahora y por siempre. Amén.

The Lord's Prayer (Ojibway)

Weosimigoyun Ishpimį eyayun,
Ta–kichituawendagwut kid ijinikazowin.
Kid ogimawiwin ta–bi–taguishinomagut.
Enendumun ta–ijiwebut oma aki tibishko iwidi ishpimį.
Mijishinam non gom gijiguk endaso–gikiguk ge–midjiya.
Gaye abueyenimishinam iniu ni muji–ijiwebizi wininanin
Eji–abueyenimungidwa igui, ga–mujidodawiyungidjig.
Gaye kego ijiwijishikangen ima gaguedibendjigewinį.
Midagwenishinam eta ima muji ayiwishį;
Kin mawin ki dibendan iu ogimawiwin,
Gaye mushkawiziwin, gaye dush iu bishigendagoziwin,
kaginig gaye kaginig. Amen.

The Lord's Prayer (Navajo/Diné)

NihiTaa' yá' aashdi holilóónii,
Nizhí' diyingo 'óólzin le',
Bee 'nóhólnúihgo bił haz' áanii baa hóya'.
Bee' íininizinii táá yá aashdi
     áanilígi át' éego,
Nahasdzáán bikáa' gi 'áánił.
Ch'iyáán t'áá 'ákwíí jí
niha' iyíłtsódíí jí nihaa
náá diní' aah;
'Áadóó baahági'ádei'nílígíí
   nihaa náhidí' aah,
T'áá nihich'į' baahági ''át'éego;

'Áadóó nihi hodínóotahjí
t'áadoo 'anihiyí' éshí,
Ndi baahági' át'éii bits' áádóó
yisdánihiyíí̜.
Háala 'aláahgo bee 'óholníigo
Bił haz 'áanii dóó bee 'adziilii
'inda bee' ayóó' ét' éii
hool' áágóó 'éí ni. Amen.

The Lord's Prayer (Chinese)

主禱文　The Lord's Prayer
我們在天上的父，
願祢的名被尊為聖，
願祢的國降臨，
願祢的旨意行在地上，
如同行在天上。
我們日用的飲食，
求父今天賜給我們。
又求饒恕我們的罪，
如同我們饒恕得罪我們的人。
不叫我們遇見試探，
拯救我們脫離凶惡。
因為國度，權柄，榮耀，
全是父的，
永無窮盡。
阿們。

The Lord's Prayer (Creole)

Papa nou ki nan syèl la
Respè anpil pou non w'
Vini tabli gouvènman w'.
Se pou volonte w' fèt toupatou
Kote moun ap viv.
Pen nou bezwen chak jou a
Bannou li Jodi a
Padonnen tout mal nou fè
Menm jan n' pran mezi n'
Pou padonnen moun ki fè n' mal tou.
Pa kite nou tonbe nan pyèj,
Wete n' anba pouvwa mal.
Paske tout pouvwa
Paske tout louwanj, tout glwa se pa w'
Depi tout tan ak pou tot tan. Amen!

Other Favorites

There is a book called *You are Special*, by Max Lucado. It's about a puppet that was treated badly because he was different. He was made fun of for his unique qualities. One day he went to the creator and the creator reminded him that being unique is a good thing. I use this book when I need a "pick-me-up." It reminds me that God made me unique and he will always love me.

Mariah Payne, Newark, Delaware

Whenever I am stressed, I like to read the book *Siddhartha*, because it is a book that reminds me of my own spiritual journey that brings me closer to God.

Randy Callender, St. Philip's Episcopal Church, Annapolis, Maryland

Rule of Life
Creator God we acknowledge and give thanks that:
In Jesus we know we belong to a Sacred Circle
    with the Gospel and Baptismal Covenant in the Center.
In this Sacred Circle:
    We are all related:
    We live a compassionate and generous life;
    We respect all life, traditions, and resources;
    We commit ourselves to spiritual growth, discipleship,
      and consensus.

A Disciple's Prayer Book

Go-To Books

An African Prayer Book by Desmond Tutu (Doubleday, 1995).

The Book of Uncommon Prayer by Stephen L. Case (Zondervan, 2002).

Call on Me: A Prayer Book for Young People by Jenifer C. Gamber and Sharon Ely Pearson (Morehouse Publishing, 2012).

A Celtic Primer edited and compiled by Brendan O'Malley (Morehouse Publishing, 2002).

Common English Bible: Life Gear for Grads (2010). www.commonenglishbible.com

Devociones del Pueblo de Dios (Forward Movement, 2013).

A Disciple's Prayer Book from the Office of Native Ministries and Gospel-Based Discipleship (Episcopal Church Center, 2003).

Gifts of Many Cultures: Worship Resources for the Global Community by Maren C. Tirabassi and Kathy Wonson Eddy (United Church Press, 1995).

God of My Heart: A Prayer Book for Youth, 2nd edition compiled and edited by Connie Wlaschin Ruhlman and Shannon Ferguson Kelly (Morehouse Education Resources, 2012).

Guide My Feet: Prayers and Meditations on Loving and Working with Children by Marian Wright Edelman (Beacon Press, 1995).

The Hip Hop Prayer Book by Timothy Holder (Church Publishing, 2006).

The Message//Remix: The Bible in Contemporary Language by Eugene Peterson (Tyndale House, 2011).

My Faith, My Life: A Teen's Guide to The Episcopal Church, 2nd edition by Jenifer C. Gamber (Morehouse Publishing, 2014).

Prayer at Night's Approaching by Jim Cotter (Morehouse Publishing, 1997).

Prayers for a Privileged People by Walter Brueggemann (Abingdon Press, 2008).

Prayers for an Inclusive Church by Steven Shakespeare (Church Publishing, 2009).

Race and Prayer: Collected Voices, Many Dreams edited by Malcolm Boyd and Bishop Chester Talton (Morehouse Publishing, 2003).

The Saint Helena Breviary The Order of Saint Helena (Church Publishing, 2006).

School Chapel Services & Prayers compiled and edited by Scott E. Ericson, St. Paul's School in Concord, New Hampshire (Church Publishing, 2007).

Sleeping with Bread: Holding What Gives You Life by Dennis Linn, Sheila Fabricant Linn and Matthew Linn (Paulist Press, 1995).

A Traveler's Prayer Book by Christopher L. Webber (Church Publishing, 1999).

A Wee Worship Book from the Wild Goose Worship Group (GIA Publications, 1999).

Go-To Websites

d365.org – daily devotions from Passport, Inc., a partnership
between The Episcopal Church, the Presbyterian Church,
and Cooperative Baptist Fellowship: www.d365.org

The Daily Office (in English and Spanish) from the Mission of
St. Clare: www.missionstclare.com

Faith Lens – weekly bible studies from the Evangelical Lutheran
Church of American (ELCA): http://blogs.elca.org/faith-
lens/

Pray as You Go – daily devotions from Jesuit Media Initiatives,
following the practice of Ignatian prayer:
www.pray-as-you-go.org/home/

Sacred Space – daily prayers in numerous languages from the
Irish Jesuits: www.sacredspace.ie